Remain

IN SEARCH OF MEDIA

Götz Bachmann, Timon Beyes, Mercedes Bunz,
and Wendy Hui Kyong Chun, Series Editors

Pattern Discrimination

Markets

Communication

Machine

Remain

Remain

Ioana B. Jucan, Jussi Parikka,
and Rebecca Schneider

IN SEARCH OF MEDIA

University of Minnesota Press
Minneapolis
London

meson press

In Search of Media is a collaboration between the
University of Minnesota Press and meson press,
an open access publisher, https://meson.press/.

Remain by Ioana B. Jucan, Jussi Parikka, and Rebecca
Schneider is licensed under a Creative Commons Attribution-
NonCommercial 4.0 International License.

Published by the
University of Minnesota Press, 2019
111 Third Avenue South, Suite 290
Minneapolis, MN 55401-2520
https://www.upress.umn.edu

in collaboration with
meson press
Salzstrasse 1
21335 Lüneburg, Germany
https://meson.press

ISBN 978-1-5179-0648-1 (pb)
A Cataloging-in-Publication record for this book is available
from the Library of Congress.

The University of Minnesota is an equal-opportunity educator
and employer.

Contents

Series Foreword   vii

Introduction: Remain × Remain(s)   ix
Ioana B. Jucan

[1]   **Remain(s) Scattered   1**
Jussi Parikka

[2]   **Slough Media   49**
Rebecca Schneider

Authors   108

Series Foreword

"Media determine our situation," Friedrich Kittler infamously wrote in his Introduction to *Gramophone, Film, Typewriter.* Although this dictum is certainly extreme—and media archaeology has been critiqued for being overly dramatic and focused on technological developments—it propels us to keep thinking about media as setting the terms for which we live, socialize, communicate, organize, do scholarship, et cetera. After all, as Kittler continued in his opening statement almost thirty years ago, our situation, "in spite or because" of media, "deserves a description." What, then, are the terms—the limits, the conditions, the periods, the relations, the phrases—of media? And, what is the relationship between these terms and determination? This book series, *In Search of Media,* answers these questions by investigating the often elliptical "terms of media" under which users operate. That is, rather than produce a series of explanatory keyword-based texts to describe media practices, the goal is to understand the conditions (the "terms") under which media is produced, as well as the ways in which media impacts and changes these terms.

Clearly, the rise of search engines has fostered the proliferation and predominance of keywords and terms. At the same time, it has changed the very nature of keywords, since now any word and pattern can become "key." Even further, it has transformed the very process of learning, since search presumes that, (a) with the right phrase, any question can be answered and (b) that the answers lie within the database. The truth, in other words, is "in there." The impact of search/media on knowledge, however, goes beyond search engines. Increasingly, disciplines—from sociology to economics, from the arts to literature—are in search of media as a way to revitalize their methods and objects of study. Our current media situation therefore seems to imply a new term, understood as temporal shifts of mediatic conditioning. Most broadly, then, this series asks: What are the terms or conditions of knowledge itself?

To answer this question, each book features interventions by two (or more) authors, whose approach to a term—to begin with: *communication, pattern discrimination, markets, remain, machine*— diverge and converge in surprising ways. By pairing up scholars from North America and Europe, this series also advances media theory by obviating the proverbial "ten year gap" that exists across language barriers due to the vagaries of translation and local academic customs. The series aims to provoke new descriptions, prescriptions, and hypotheses—to rethink and reimagine what media can and must do.

Remain × Remain(s)

Ioana B. Jucan

> History is time that won't quit.
> —Suzan-Lori Parks

What remains in the wake of centuries of technological and scientific developments and in the wake of histories of modern progress—which is also to say histories of dispossession, displacement, and exploitation? How are remains and remainders, and the process of remaining, to be understood, engaged, and entered into a relationship with? What is the place of remain(s) in a global capitalist, consumerist culture that is constantly rushing after the next "new" thing on the market? What and where are the leftovers of this culture, and how do "we" (consumers of the new) live with what we leave behind? How is the past that is not past, subject as it has been to denials and erasures, to be engaged and lived with—and through? What is the matter and temporality of remains? And why and how does what remains matter?

Through their complex relations to times and spaces that are plural and nonhomogeneous, "remain(s)" accumulate a multiplicity of meanings and open a multiplicity of possibilities of thought and (re)encounter. The two essays in this book, by Rebecca Schneider and Jussi Parikka, gesture toward some of these meanings and enact some of these possibilities. This introduction aims to point to an open interval of conversation and exchange between them. Taking my cue from Schneider's and Parikka's essays, I begin with a diagram that seeks to stage some of the possibilities of thought gathered around the concept of *remain* used as a verb, noun, call (hail, imperative), state, or process of becoming.

The authors of this book approach the question of remain(s) from the directions of their inherently interdisciplinary fields of scholarship: theater and performance studies (Schneider) and media studies—more specifically, media archaeology (Parikka). Remarking that performance studies "resists a definitive delimitation," Schneider (2007) proposed in an interview to think performance studies—particularly, performance studies in its ampersand relation to theater and theatricality—as "an invitation to put ideas into play" and as "a wonderful arena for thinking about cross-temporal engagements." Some of the ideas that she has put into play in her work—in different shapes and in relation to a wide range of concerns—are those of "cross-temporal liveness" (Schneider 2007); the "undecidable space between registers of what is live and what is passed," on which theater has a "particular purchase" (Schneider 2012, 155; see also Schneider 2011); and—through the concept of "intrainanimation"—"the ways the dead play across the bodies of the living, and the living replay the dead" (Schneider 2017). In *What Is Media Archaeology?*, Parikka (2012, 2, 4, 5) wrote that media archaeology (as approached and practiced in his book) "offers an insight into *how to think media archaeologically* in contemporary culture" and proposed that this mode of thinking start from the premise of "the entanglement of past and present." Elsewhere, he wrote about media archaeology as "executed media philosophies of time" and as "a method for excavation of the repressed, the forgotten, or the past" as well as "an artistic method close to DIY culture, circuit bending, hardware hacking, and other exercises that intervene the political economy of information technology" (Parikka 2015, 7; Hertz and Parikka 2015, 142). One direction in which Parikka has explored the complexity of the entanglements

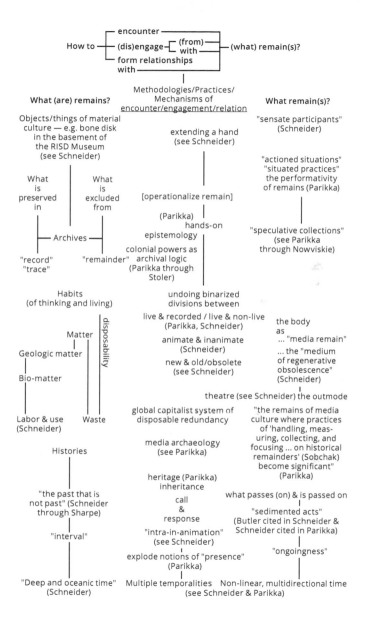

How to — encounter / (dis)engage — (from) / with — form relationships with — (what) remain(s)?

Methodologies/Practices/Mechanisms of encounter/engagement/relation

What (are) remains?

Objects/things of material culture — e.g. bone disk in the basement of the RISD Museum (see Schneider)

What is preserved in — Archives — What is excluded from

"record" "trace" — "remainder"

extending a hand (see Schneider)

[operationalize remain]

(Parikka) hands-on epistemology

colonial powers as archival logic (Parikka through Stoler)

What remain(s)?

"sensate participants" (Schneider)

"actioned situations" "situated practices" the performativity of remains (Parikka)

"speculative collections" (see Parikka through Nowviskie)

Habits (of thinking and living)

Matter
Geologic matter
Bio-matter

disposability

Labor & use (Schneider) Waste

undoing binarized divisions between

live & recorded / live & non-live (Parikka, Schneider)

animate & inanimate (Schneider)

new & old/obsolete (see Schneider)

the body as
... "media remain"
... the "medium of regenerative obsolescence" (Schneider)

theatre (see Schneider) the outmode

global capitalist system of disposable redundancy

"the remains of media culture where practices of 'handling, measuring, collecting, and focusing ... on historical remainders' (Sobchak) become significant" (Parikka)

Histories

"the past that is not past" (Schneider through Sharpe)

"interval"

media archaeology (see Parikka)

heritage (Parikka) inheritance

call & response

"intra-in-animation" (see Schneider)

explode notions of "presence" (Parikka)

what passes (on) & is passed on

"sedimented acts" (Butler cited in Schneider & Schneider cited in Parikka)

"ongoingness"

"Deep and oceanic time" (Schneider)

Multiple temporalities

Non-linear, multidirectional time (see Schneider & Parikka)

of pasts, presents, and futures is that of *A Geology of Media,* where he focuses on "the literal deep times and deep places of media in mines and rare earth minerals" and on the earth as an "archive" of a variety of technological and chemical traces often constituted as residues/waste (Parikka 2015, 5, x). This inquiry into "a geology of media" intersects with media ecology, the latter of which refers to "the concrete connections that media as technology has to resources . . . and nature" (Parikka 2013, 75).

Notably, Parikka's and Schneider's different approaches to remain(s) intersect in the kind of thinking—and (re)conceptualization—of time and matter that, they seem to imply, an engagement with the epistemological and ontological complexity of remain(s) calls for. "The remain is not something neatly placed on the linear scale of old and new," writes Parikka in his essay. Instead of this binary old–new option, he proposes addressing "the urgency of the remainder as a question that can be tackled in media theory as a mapping of *heterochronia.*" The latter concept brings into focus the "multiple temporalities" entangled around (what) remain(s) as well as the remains' distributed "locatability." Connecting technology's thrall to newness and "Western history's linear time-machine" to modernity's "so-called march of progress" (Schneider, this volume), Schneider too thinks remain(s) outside of the binarized distinction between new and old. In (what I call) the capitalist system of disposable redundancy, the (planned, programmed) production of the new is in equal measure the production of the obsolete. As Schneider phrases it, through Wendy Chun, "each so-called new is essentially the new outmode according to habit." Despite modernity's fantasy of erasing the old so as to construct the (purely) new, the outmode does not go away—it only goes elsewhere. Or, in Parikka's (2015, 141) words from *A Geology of Media,* "obsolescence returns"—and remains. In the appendix of that book, featuring an essay written together with Garnet Hertz titled "Zombie Media: Circuit Bending Media Archaeology into an Art Method," Parikka engages the concept of "planned obsolescence," initially proposed by Bernard London as a solution for ending the Great Depression.

Hertz and Parikka (2015, 142) remark that, "far from being acciden-
tal, discarding and obsolescence are in fact internal to contemporary media technologies."

To build off Parikka's thoughts, discarding and obsolescence are in
fact internal to the capitalist mode of production and consumption
more broadly, which both produces and feeds off the habit of disposability. A paradigmatic embodiment of this habit is disposable
plastics, which Parikka evokes through Kristina Lindström and Åsa
Ståhl's *Plastic Imaginaries.* Schneider too evokes disposable plastics
as the "strangely non-vanishing secret of obsolescence" (through
Boyan Slat, CEO of the Ocean Cleanup). As historian Jeffrey Meikle
(1995, 190) explains in *American Plastic*, by 1950, "an endemic
oversupply" of plastics left over from the war "led producers to
think not of durability but of disposability" in relation to plastic, and
to market it as a valueless thing meant for limited—often single—
use, a thing produced to be discarded. Since 1940, not only plastics
but also everything that is caught up in this system has arguably
come to be treated as disposable. This includes human beings (or
"human resources"), whose subjectivity—modeled on plasticity as
flexibility, adaptability, and an obsession with the new (as the latest
thing on the market)—is (re)produced, sold, and bought (again and
again) as part of the game of relentless profit making.

But there is a long history to disposability that extends much
further than the 1930s and 1940s emergence of "planned obsolescence" as a driving principle in the consumer market. This history
is still at work. It is a history in which capitalism and colonialism—
both systems of appropriation and exploitation of land and labor
(see also Wolfe 2016)—have been inextricably intertwined, as
Schneider reminds us in her essay, citing Glen Coulthard. At the
core of this intertwining are the institution of slavery and the dispossession, displacement, and elimination of indigenous peoples.
In his book *Traces of History,* where he argues that "race is a trace of
history," Patrick Wolfe (2016, 3) traces different regimes of race and
logics of racialization and the different yet related histories with
which they are associated. These are, more specifically, "a history

of bodily exploitation" in the case of enslaved populations and "one of territorial dispossession" in the case of indigenous populations. In the case of both these threads of histories, "the pernicious logics of racialization" has been in the business of rendering disposable "numerous individuals and populations around the globe"—and it continues to do so, in the name of white supremacy (Weheliye 2014, 15). These histories, of slavery and of colonial dispossessions and erasures, remain. They remain in different ways—of being, doing, and thinking.

A correlate of thinking remain(s) outside/beside modernity's linear conception of forward-marching time is that "the past, then, is not past, nor is the future future" (Maurice Merleau-Ponty, as cited in Schneider, this volume) and that "the past that is not past reappears" (Christina Sharpe, as cited in Schneider, this volume). In her book *In the Wake,* Christina Sharpe (2016, 53) asks: "[H]ow does one memorialize chattel slavery and its afterlives, which are unfolding still? How do we memorialized an event that is still ongoing?" This notion—of the *ongoingness,* the unfolding, of a past that is not past—is key to the thinking of (what) remain(s), and it appears prominently, in different forms, both in Schneider and in Parikka's essays.

Schneider stages "an ongoing, deep time, *live* scene" of encounter with a bone disk artifact in the basement of the Rhode Island School of Design Museum. This is, in Schneider's words, a "scene of extended circulation," stretching through "cross-temporal exchange" to the Roman Empire; it is, in her words again, "a scene of significant duration, spanning millennia, in which this bit of bone has been passed hand to hand to hand and in which hands have reached out to receive it." Schneider unfolds this scene through the trope, gesture, and practice of "extending a hand." Thinking extension as in-hand brings attention to what moves off the hand and what passes from hand to hand across temporal and spatial intervals. It also attends to the modes of repeating, preserving, and hailing that happen through this kind of "handwork" that is inextricably tied to "iterability." And it attends to the "call and response that weaves past and future in intervallic resonance" and the "response-ability" that comes with it, both in the sense of calling "the past to appear for account" and of being called by "the past to respond with account."

The work of nonlinear, multidirectional time takes place in and through matter, and matter embodies the work—or (differently articulated) bears the weight—of time. As used here, "matter" is plural, heterogeneous, differentiated into a multiplicity of beings and ways of being—and it is a matter of relation. "Extending a hand," as Schneider theorizes it, attends to the work of time through/in plural matter, to matters of circulation and relation. Challenging binarized divisions between animate and inanimate, between live and not-live, and between human and nonhuman, Schneider conjoins the concept of "extending a hand" with that of "intrainanimation" (derived from Fred Moten and John Donne as well as from Karen Barad and Donna Haraway). This concept shifts the emphasis "off of a generalized claim about the animacy of everything" (a claim made in certain strands of new materialist writings)[1] "onto the idea of interstitial relations across varieties of heterogeneous beings engaging in call and response." As it moves from the scene of the encounter with the bone disk to the "Savage Curtain" episode from the third season of *Star Trek* (and back, in various directions and senses), Schneider's essay enacts, it seems to me, this very idea. The idea has ethical and political implications, toward which Schneider gestures when she asks, "How can we approach the *matter* of intrainanimacy with respect for all lifeways that circulate among us all, across vast stretches of time, vast stretches of space as well as at the tiniest increment of a single quivering leaf or bit of detritus of bone?"

In conversation with Parikka's "turn to mineral and chemical matter as geologic remains of media," and with his statement that "media starts much *before media becomes media,*" Schneider focuses in particular on what she terms "the *performance* remains of media"—more specifically, "bio-matter" ("the live body") and "geologic matter" as "prehistorical matter of media." Her interest is in "the in-handedness of media," in the ways in which the live body, "flesh and bone," as well as the "labor and use" (the latter understood to include "rituals, habits, and encounters") with which they are associated, are media components and mediatic remains, perhaps "pre-historic" ones. In this way of thinking media and the body, media are not "the extensions of man" (as Marshal McLuhan [2013] proclaimed); rather, the body is "itself *already* mediatic," itself a "means to extension" and, thus, a means of relationality and circulation.

Engaging the question of (what) remain(s) from the direction of media archaeology, Parikka too thinks remain(s) in terms of relationality. He emphasizes becoming as a mode of remaining, a mode that is "situated in particular spaces of making/thinking but also in historical situations" (Parikka, this volume). Giving particular attention to archives and archiving, to what gets preserved and what excluded in the constitution of archives, his approach is to "operationalize remain," to take it as "an active formation, a situated practice." Through this approach, in his words again, "the remain(s) become more of an event that summons new relations and potentials than merely a thing to be classified; it expands outside its cabinets, classifications and index systems to the histories, archaeological sediments, and the great outdoors from which it comes from."

Parikka highlights the Media Archaeological Fundus as an example of "a place where the relation to remains is staged." Hosted by media theorist Wolfgang Ernst at Humboldt University in Berlin (Germany), the Fundus is "a collection of various electromechanical and mechanical artefacts as they developed throughout time"; the aim of the Fundus is "to provide a perspective that may inspire modern thinking about technology and media within its epistemological implications beyond bare historiography."[2] The artifacts in the collection are to be engaged "hands-on," in a way that resonates with "the work of critical making." Parikka refers to this performative mode of engagement with the collection in terms of a "*hands*-on epistemology" (emphasis added). As Parikka notes, "the hands that are operating, pointing, opening up a remain of a thing become partial agents in this play" and in the videos from the Fundus. In ways that resonate with Schneider's theorization of hand and body, Parikka thinks of hands as something of an "obsolete sort of a remainder" and of "the body as a sort of a threshold—not a celebration of the human body, but a mobilization of its possibilities as part of the thresholds, interfaces that move across scales, and make the body already something else than it is." Yet, even as they share a dynamic understanding of the archival and as they "move beyond oppositions of live and documented, live and recorded, to the productive liveness of the archival as an embodied situation," "hands-on epistemology" and Schneider's "extending a hand" differ notably. As discussed earlier, for Schneider, "extending a hand" is a matter of what moves *off* the hand in scenes of exchange and circulation that take place across temporal and spatial intervals spanning significant durations. This is different from the idea of manipulating remains in a lab space, albeit "technologically 'infected' humanities labs" (Stefan Höltgen, as cited in Parikka, this volume).

Thinking with Ernst, Parikka writes that, in this kind of hands-on engagement with collections as "hybrid sites of learning, theory and to some extent collecting," the artifacts are "not props for a writing of a historical narrative but production of history that is itself executed in place." For Ernst, this idea of the artifacts not being props for writing a historical narrative implies "radically de-historicizing the archive" (as the title of one of his essays reads) through media archeological approaches. In the case of digitized archives, an example of a media archeological approach would be to apply "creative algorithms to experiment with new forms of navigating enormous amounts of archival signals and data" (Ernst 2016, 10). Ernst's goal for the kind of dehistoricization that he proposes is to decouple the modern archive from the "territorial nation state" and from narrative (11). However, by focusing exclusively on technical–mathematical operations, the kind of dehistoricization he proposes, it seems to me, risks to evacuate the social and to participate in (further) erasures of histories, which "official" (colonial and colonized) archives have relentlessly perpetrated.

The erasures, gaps, or silences in the archive, too, (are) remain(s), forms of the past that is not past. Saidiya Hartman, for instance, writes about the "silence in the archive" in relation to the archive of Atlantic slavery and about the violence of this archive. How is one to engage this silence and the constitutive violence of this archive? "Straining against the limits of the archive to write a cultural history of the captive, and, at the same time, enacting the impossibility of representing the lives of the captives precisely through the process of narration," Hartman (2008, 11) proposes the method of "critical fabulation" in her essay "Venus in Two Acts." This method, as she practices it, writes Hartman, involves "playing with and rearranging the basic elements of the story, . . . representing the sequence of events in divergent stories and from contested points of view" (11), without, however, giving up narrative altogether. In Hartman's words again, "the outcome of this method is a 'recombinant narrative,' which loops the strands of incommensurate accounts and which weaves present, past, and future in retelling the girl's [Venus's] story and in narrating the time of slavery as our present" (12).

Departing from Ernst while keeping his stance in perspective as one set of possibilities of operationalizing remains, Parikka goes on to think hands-on epistemology in the direction of "speculative collections," a concept he borrows from Bethany Nowviskie (2016), who in turn took inspiration "from theory and practice in Afrofuturism and other forms of speculative art and design, from the concepts of kairos and temporal modeling, the Caribbean 'otherwise,' a striving toward 'impossible archival imaginaries' and 'usable pasts,' and from emancipatory research, a notion of 'archival liveness,' and the ethics of care." Like Hartman's "critical fabulation," "speculative collections" take seriously "the gaps and uncertainties" in and of the archive (Nowviskie 2016). Hartman's (2008, 3) focus is on the question of "how does one rewrite the chronicle of a death foretold and anticipated, as a collective biography of dead subjects, as a counter-history of the human, as the practice of freedom." Relatedly, yet with a somewhat different emphasis, the driving question of Afrofuturism, as cyberculture critic Mark Dery (as cited in Nowviskie 2016) formulates it, is, how "can a community whose past has been deliberately rubbed out . . . imagine possible futures?" Working in the fields of digital scholarship and digital cultural heritage, Nowviskie takes inspiration from "the Afrofuturist notion of cultural heritage not as content to be received but technology to be used," and asks, "How do you position digital collections and digital scholarly projects not as statements about what was, but as toolsets and resources for what could be?"

In his essay from this volume, Parikka takes the idea of "cultural heritage not as content to be received but as technology to be used" in different directions and areas of practice—specifically, those of (media) arts and design—with a particular focus on questions of infrastructure (and the labor it takes to build it) as well as on "a wider ecology of remains." As he pursues these questions, he brings attention, among other things, to "possible toxic legacies of technological culture" and to "possibilities of reuse of materials." Toxicity, which spreads (contamination) both spatially and temporally, remains and, in its remaining, troubles any binary division between so-called animate and so-called inanimate matter. Schneider touches on this idea, too, in relation to the "queer intimacy" between mineral and live body in the experience of "mercury poisoning" recounted in Mel Y. Chen's *Animacies: Biopolitics, Racial Mattering, and Queer Affect.* Toxicity is thus another form of ongoingness, of the "unfolding" (to repeat a term that Parikka uses often) of remains playing out across extended temporal and spatial intervals and scales. Across such intervals and scales, much (else) remains to think through, respond to, handle, care for, relate to. The essays that follow unfold some of these remains.

Notes

1 See, e.g., Jane Bennett's (2010) *Vibrant Matter.*
2 This description is taken from web page about the Media Archaeological Fundus hosted on the website of Humboldt University, accessible at https://www.musikundmedien.hu-berlin.de/de/medienwissenschaft/medientheorien/fundus/media-archaeological-fundus.

References

Bennett, Jane. 2010. *Vibrant Matter: A Political Ecology of Things.* Durham, N.C.: Duke University Press.

Ernst, Wolfgang. 2016. "Radically De-historicizing the Archive." In *Decolonising Archives.* L'Internationale Online. http://www.internationaleonline.org/bookshelves /decolonising_archives.

Hartman, Saidiya. 2008. "Venus in Two Acts." *Small Axe: A Caribbean Journal of Criticism* 26: 1–14.

Hertz, Garnet, and Jussi Parikka. 2015. "Appendix: Zombie Media: Circuit Bending Media Archaeology into an Art Method." In *A Geology of Media,* pp. 141–53. Minneapolis: University of Minnesota Press.

McLuhan, Marshall. 2013. *Understanding Media: The Extensions of Man.* New York: Gingko Press.

Meikle, Jeffrey. 1995. *American Plastic: A Cultural History.* New Brunswick, N.J.: Routledge.

Nowviskie, Bethany. 2016. *Speculative Collections.* October 27. http://nowviskie.org/ 2016/speculative-collections/.

Parikka, Jussi. 2012. *What Is Media Archeology?* Cambridge: Polity Press.

Parikka, Jussi. 2013. "Green Media Times: Friedrich Kittler and Ecological Media History." In *Mediengeschichte nach Friedrich Kittler, edited by Friedrich Balke, Bernhard Siegert, and Joseph Vogl,* pp. 69–78. Munich, Germany: Wilhelm Fink.

Parikka, Jussi. 2015. *A Geology of Media.* Minneapolis: University of Minnesota Press.

Schneider, Rebecca. 2007. "Interview with Rebecca Schneider." In *What Is Performance Studies?* http://scalar.usc.edu/nehvectors/wips/rebecca-schneider-what-is -performance-studies-2007.

Schneider, Rebecca. 2011. *Performing Remains: Art and War in Times of Theatrical Reenactment.* New York: Routledge.

Schneider, Rebecca. 2012. "It Seems as If . . . I Am Dead: Zombie Capitalism and Theatrical Labor." *The Drama Review* 56, no. 4: 150–62.

Schneider, Rebecca, in conversation with Lucia Ruprecht. 2017. "In Our Hands: An Ethics of Gestural Response-ability." *Performance Philosophy* 3, no. 1. http://www .performancephilosophy.org/journal/article/view/161/172.

Sharpe, Christina. 2016. *In the Wake: On Blackness and Being.* Durham, N.C.: Duke University Press.

Weheliye, Alexander. 2014. *Habeas Viscus: Racializing Assemblages, Biopolitics, and Black Feminist Theories of the Human.* Durham, N.C.: Duke University Press.

Wolfe, Patrick. 2016. *Traces of History: Elementary Structures of Race.* London: Verso.

Remain(s) Scattered

Jussi Parikka

The Primacy of the Remainder

John Akomfrah and Trevor Mathison's *All That Is Solid* is an investigation into the ephemeral afterlife of voice and sound. Subtitled *The Discreet Afterlife of Auditory Objects,* it looks and listens into the aesthetic, and difficult, task of conceiving history as an archival reality that folds into an unreality of things that fade away. The film achieves this by shifting images of fog and other environing situations that tell a story of a temporal fading that is not merely "decay" in the usual sense, as the term is used in relation to issues of memory and the archive. "History is scattered" is one leading line of the film, and it is a perfect way of leading into a discussion of remains—what remains, and a remainder of things material. What does it mean to think the remains beyond the discrete documented remains and as part of a more alive, embodied, and event-based performative (Schneider 2011, 87–110)? The remains are both in place and yet distributed; they are material and sometimes foggy. They can be a mood and an environment, even if sometimes coming out as an object categorized in institutional situations. It can be the infrastructure that bootstraps us as part of what remained, although this wider scale of remains has not always been the key focus of a cultural heritage discourse. What remained is also a question of where remained: what set of places pertain to remains,

[Figure 1.1.] John Akomfrah, *All That Is Solid,* 2015, single-channel HD color video, 5.1 sound, 29 minutes 52 seconds. Copyright Smoking Dogs Films. Courtesy Lisson Gallery.

in what sort of institutions of memory, as well as in what sort of practices of engaging with remains?

It feels almost too obvious to say this out loud, but *remain* is one of those rather elusive words that, despite or because of this slippery nature, also attracts media theoretical attention. It becomes easily attached as part of a series of related terms: obsolescence, residuals, abandoned, forgotten, side-lined, and lost. It slips out of focus because of the seeming commonality, while it does, too, include a force of its own. It speaks to the senses and, as such, to various bodily situations in which we are somewhat faced with remains. It is no wonder that the remains of the auditory that is the focus of Akomfrah and Mathison's film is approached through things as elusive as atmospheric condensations of water that we can inhale. Fog, mist, membranes of different sorts, suitably ghostly projection surfaces in their own right, lend their own material ephemerality to that which remains.

Even if it seems sometimes out of place, as an order word, it signifies an imperative of place—remain! But more often than not, it actually implies the unruly movement of bits and bops, of fragments and residues that do not remain in their place. No wonder things appear misty. As scattered, it bothers and escapes, slips and vanishes. While the remains seem out of place, there is a place of remainders; furthermore, "remain" as a concept and as a practice has a material spatiality in humanities disciplines such as media archaeology. The archival remains always have a topology; they are addressable to a place (cf. Schneider 2011, 107–8). But also at large, we can approach the remain(s) as part of wider questions of design and infrastructure, of pasts and obsolescence in the present, contemporary now. Where does the remain remain, to whom does it remain, and how does it remain as an active presence that demands a relation to it? To remain is not merely a passive state of what happened to remain but can be an active relation through which to think issues of temporality but also issues of production of cultural reality. Is the remainder only the obsolete, or could it be slightly something more living? This is also why the question of the remain(s) as it is posed by media theorists and scholars of the archive benefit from a close dialogue with theorists of performance (see Schneider, this volume; see also Schneider 2011). Rebecca Schneider speaks of slough media—an aptly durational concept for the work of remaining that pertains both to people and to things, to bodies and their material contexts of intra-activity.

But first to put things in order, even if one is aware how easily they are uncontained and leak. The term *remain(s)* is itself, rather recursively, a prime example of a remainder. It reminds of the difficulty of any universal classification system supposed to operate without ambiguity and without a disturbing remainder of that which is left out, or that which overlaps and disturbs the smooth epistemological coherence. It is not that such systems have not been planned. We know that from the history of science and media that could be read as varied epistemotheological takes on trying to get rid of the remainder and toward encompassing knowledge of the world from Aristotle to the Middle Ages and the Renaissance, including Ramon Llull, Giordano Bruno, encyclopedist Johann Heinrich Alsted, theosophist Jan Amos Comenius, and the seventeenth-century clergyman and philosopher John Wilkins, not to forget the attempts for such a system in the current schemes for the ontology of the Semantic Web, as Florian Cramer (2013, 93) reminds us. There is an entire media archaeology of attempts of classification, and hence there is a whole media archaeology of failed classifications, whether the failure is acknowledged or not.

Borges famously took ridicule of the various historical examples of classification schemes in his fabulation about the imaginary case of the Chinese encyclopedia *Celestial Empire of Benevolent Knowledge*. This is the story that includes the litany of animals. It might be a well-known list, but let's remind ourselves:

> These ambiguities, redundancies and deficiencies remind us of those which doctor Franz Kuhn attributes to a certain Chinese encyclopaedia entitled "Celestial Empire of benevolent Knowledge." In its remote pages it is written that the animals are divided into: (a) belonging to the emperor, (b) embalmed, (c) tame, (d) sucking pigs, (e) sirens, (f) fabulous, (g) stray dogs, (h) included in the present classification, (i) frenzied, (j) innumerable, (k) drawn with a very fine camelhair brush, (l) et cetera, (m) having just broken the water pitcher, (n) that from a long way off look like flies. (Borges, as quoted in Cramer 2013, 94)

Such examples are apt in how they show the fact that any classifications and their remainders are always produced; they take place as historical hinges around which knowledge crystallizes, clusters, is organized and defined, but also the question as to what are the conditions of this particular operation of knowledge forming. Remains are always in relation to what did not remain and what defined the borders of inclusion and exclusion. Michel Foucault picked up on this, as did, indeed, did Cramer (2013, 96). He reminds that such epistemological models, or productions, operate in the context of the Semantic Web and that in the background of any knowledge system and what can and cannot "be mapped into computer data structures except in subjective, diverse, cultural controversial and folksonomic ways."

Besides a classificatory nightmare and/or an obsession, one can pay attention to the subtleties of the term *remain*—and what it *does* to our understanding of culture and media in a variety of ways that hopefully would make Derrida proud and Foucault happily sigh with a sense of accomplishment, thinking to themselves, "they took seriously the point that its not only the archive but also what is excluded, what defies the categories and shows the contingent cultural techniques that actually define what remains, what not, and what's a remainder." The double meaning of *remain* is that which is left behind as enduring legacy that is archived but also that which is *left out* of the classification or the archive. In other words, to remain and the remainder can paradoxically refer to what is being left as acknowledged but also as the unacknowledged. This is at the same time the rather central problem of the archival a priori in the sense that the archive is supposed to be the ruling condition of history, while itself historical; a condition of writing what remained while itself setting itself as the epistemological defining threshold of remainders (Winthrop-Young 2015, 145).

One could continue for a longer period and for several more pages on the media epistemological conditions of the archive, and there is plenty of literature on this archival condition as the condition of knowledge (see, e.g., Derrida 1995; Ebeling and Günzel 2009; Eichhorn 2013; Ernst 2013; Schneider 2011). There is also the context in which such questions illustrate how colonial powers work as archival logic. Ann Stoler details in her *Along the Archival Grain* in fabulous ways the grim operations of colonial institutions and how archives participate in production of social categories. Stoler (2009, 1) brings to the fore how the Dutch colonialists handled slippery, unclassifiable material in their colonial archives:

Grids of intelligibility were fashioned from uncertain knowledge; disquiet and anxieties registered the uncommon sense of events and things; epistemic uncertainties repeatedly unsettled the imperial conceit that all was in order, because papers classified people, because directives were properly acknowledged, and because colonial civil servants were schooled to assure that records were prepared, circulated, securely stored, and sometimes rendered to ash.

Stoler's book demonstrates how an effective way of handling complex information is to classify it—both by way of rendering those systems of intelligibility and by way of also classifying as top secret, inaccessible. This can be seen as a way to hide the remainder and the questionable troubling bits that would also challenge the legitimacy of the system's rationality[1]—the particular discrete document that traces a history of what lends itself to be inscribed as part of the particular topology of the archive and what are the "lost histories" (Schneider 2011, 99) of minorities and Others?

Acknowledging the importance of the postcolonial analyses, as well as the media epistemological questions of "remains" that constantly remain on the agenda, as well as, for example, the media archaeological connotations that I will address a bit later, I want to operationalize the term. What does it mean to take *remain* as an active formation, a situated practice, even if scattered across institutional contexts, art and curatorial discourses, infrastructural pipelines and media archaeological techniques? I want to mobilize the concept toward ends that show how *remain* is a term that opens up toward situated practices of encountering remains. This is where the dialogue with performance studies becomes especially fruitful (see, again, Schneider, this volume).

Besides the performative, embodied dimension, a particular focus on the conditions of remains becomes a way of exploding the notion of presence of a thing or a document into a multiplicity of time. The remain is not something neatly placed on the linear scale of old and new—something that Lisa Parks (2007) early on reminded is a rather unfulfilling way of approaching media history. Instead of such binary options, we can address the urgency of the remainder as a question that can be tackled in media theory as a mapping of *heterochronia* (see Winthrop-Young 2015). This term refers to the multiple temporalities that media archaeological theory has introduced and, more widely, the multiple temporalities that define media culture—a situation much more complex than to speak of old/new. But this heterochronia is also a question of *where* the remains are, not a question of mere formal epistemo-ontology but a question of locatability and the distributed remains that turns to much more than just a rehashing of the archival—it turns into issues of design and material culture, of remains as *actioned situations.* This is an idea that in ways follows from some key ideas by Cornelia Vismann's take on the media history of files and archives, as well as, for example, Knut Ebeling's developments: the archive does not merely state facts; it produces events and realities, performs files and facts (Ebeling 2007, 112–13). It is this sort of a performativity that comes out gradually as a central theme of this text, too, while also then moving to scales where the performativity moves outside the singular subject: what are the infrastructural situations in which remains are or demand actions? Where are archives produced, and where do sites of history turn from archives and libraries to laboratories and other places of engaging with what remained? To rework the past becomes one sort of a practice-based look at imaginaries of archives that also expose their conditions of existence as something that leak beyond the taxonomic categories and disciplines of knowledge.

The text proceeds by way of three different sections that continue the briefly introduced engagement between conceptual and media theoretical questions concerning "remain(s)," while toward the end of the text, the focus shifts to the speculative and yet situated idea of remains. By the time we reach the end, we will have returned to the movements of remains, and hence the order word *remain!* restores the connotation with spatialities and temporalities, situation,

[Figure 1.2.] Image from the *Archive Space* exhibition, curated by Dr. Jane Birkin. Image courtesy of Special Collections, Hartley Library, University of Southampton.

place, but in the context of design, art practices, and contemporary culture. Furthermore, this essay is accompanied by a series of images that, on one level, refer to the artistic and curatorial projects that are part of the dialogue and, on another level, narrate the argument in their own right. They mark the spot of remains as

The Remains of Media

In some aspect, a remainder is somewhat like (technical) media:
it is not a poor replica of the assumed original but itself already
an event that has its own duration and existence, its own logic
and temporality, itself part of a series of situations and events. It
does not merely mark a spot of something gone but works as its
own generative force (see also Schneider, this volume). Instead of
assumed originals, in the rather Derrida-inspired sense, one can
say that the remains were *already there* and already troubled by
the difficulty of returning it to the original. The remain is not merely
secondary but the primary entry to a different temporal regime
that is still, oddly enough, persistently here as a thing but also as
something more. The emergence of the *re*-main is to be taken
as primary even if one would be tempted to think of it as a trace
that is not fully present (Derrida 2005, 151). What establishes the
remain is where it becomes embodied, too—not merely a spectral
presence but something of a taking place of history. As Schneider
(2011, 104) explains, based on Derrida, "To read 'history,' then, as a
set of sedimented acts that are not the historical acts themselves
but the act of security any incident backward—the repeated act of
securing memory—is to rethink the site of history in ritual repetition." The place becomes a central stage for this particular bundle
of repetition: the archive, the remains, the embodied performative
dimension of its existence.

While acknowledging the centrality of Derrida's *Archive Fever* and
other considerations about remains, we also have to reach out to
some other ways of engaging with the overflowing materiality of
remains, and the various imaginaries it might trigger as more, not
less, than its actuality. There's more to the remains than meets the
archival place. Remain has repetition bootstrapped into it already
as a sort of a forceful implication of the serial production taking

place that already inserted something as a remainder, as remains. That the original never just remained but multiplied and left a trace becomes an onto-epistemological challenge. This sort of an emphasis comes as part of Derrida's desire to trouble the idea of the remain as merely about the residual or the subtracted and any supposition of a linear force of time. By starting with the question of the remainder, we have already actually stepped into a question that is not about what was there originally and what remained of that assumed original but about a more fundamental sense of how such separations, differentiations, and seeming distinctions are being produced; the remainder itself contains its originals, or more accurately, could be turned as the original itself. What has remained and is here, in this place, is itself troubling.

What else if not remains of the media have tickled the fancy of so much of media studies. There has been a pronounced and sustained eagerness to discover hidden layers of cultural determinations as well as the power that operates the epistemological structures of classification. Often it comes by the name of media archaeology. *Media archaeology* is one term for the broad field where remains remain at the forefront, troubling the urgency of the supposedly new with the multiple other times that still persist: the time of the old, the obsolete, the fading, the slowly emerging, the parallel, the returning, the deep time, the time that is not reducible to a linear history. So many times. The archaeological concepts that had an impact in the psychoanalytic epistemology (Elsaesser 2011) carry a continuing weight in the context of media methodologies as well as discussions concerning the archive. Vivian Sobchak (2011) makes the case that this is a demonstration of how the transhistorical is one word for this particular approach to media culture and for the analytical ways media studies makes sense of the situation—the remains of media culture where practices of "handling, measuring, collecting and focusing . . . on historical remainders" (324) become significant as the framework for the unity of the broad field of media archaeology. For there are, of course, so many ways in which media archaeology deals with remains. The remain(s) arrive(s) in separate ways.

For example, the remainder itself is part of the history of media for the part it plays in mathematics and especially accounting. As Markus Krajewski points out, West European languages adopt the term that stems from Latin *restare* in the fifteenth century, a term that was made all the more acute with "the spread of new commercial technologies such as double-entry bookkeeping, which knows no unexpected remainders purely thanks to its logic" (Krajewski 2014, 196–97). One is tempted to say that the rest is history, that the remainder is part of a media infrastructural circuiting of material and immaterial things, whether as debit or as credit.

Alternatively, considering remains and their persistence, we can speak of how certain use practices and forms remain relevant forms even after surpassed by a seemingly more dominant media practice or apparatus. A very apt example could be found in visual media: consider it as an example of remaining, when Reynaud's optical theater sustains its status and remains popular even after the late nineteenth-century cinematic devices, such as the cinematograph, emerge (Strauven 2011, 162n21; Crary 1999, 266). And similarly, Reynaud's optical theater did not manage to get rid of the old-fashioned hand-cranked tactile forms of moving image entertainment (Strauven 2011, 157). The anecdotal example from a much larger body of work by archaeologists of the audiovisual already demonstrates that media live parallel lives that demonstrate the multiple overlapping rhythms of media, instead of merely as old or new. One could expand this to a broader geographical question, too (something we will in certain ways return to later): *where* is the old, where is the new, where else would something deemed obsolete take place as still usable (see Elsaesser 2016)?

Remains are sometimes the archival documents left for posterity, and yet sometimes even as such extra-ordinary—examples of the remains of what we don't always realize. Are the sidetracked, some even ridiculed, ideas registered from 1871 to 1946 in the Prussian Academy of Sciences special section "Worthless Submissions from the Public" the true useless remains of the emergence of scientific culture? As Markus Krajewski (2001) narrates about the collections housed at the Berlin-Brandenburg's Akademie der Wissenschaften archive, this is sort of a parallel history of public engagement with science, abundant with wild oscillations that go left field in theories of the earth, theories of gravity, a hint of what an archive of impossible media, or just an archive of bad ideas, might be. Or is this an early form of the speculative collection (Nowviskie 2016)?

One could continue the list of various examples of how remains could be thematically and methodologically tackled in media studies, but let me turn my attention to the more material instances in which remains are at the center of methodological inquiries into past and present media cultures.

In other words, remains are not merely archival in the sense of the archived document, or even as narrativized attention to persistence of media forms, but also as material, concrete, touchable, sensible objects and things. Any consideration of remain(s) and the remainder should include the wider environment, or ecology, in which it takes place. In the 2016–17 exhibition at the Level Four gallery at the Hartley Library, University of Southampton, the theme of the archive as a material reality was explicated and expanded much outside the actual object to the conditions of the environment as a spatial setting that has to do with temperatures and other settings. Curated by artist and theorist Jane Birkin, the small photograph exhibition features *Archive Spaces* that are revealed to be the spatialized, institutional version of the four elements. They come out less as mythical, nostalgic longing for ancient Greece than as particular affordances for the remains to be sustained: strong rooms to the conservation department's wet studio, smoke detection system, and volatile store with photographic negatives in the freezer. Archives are environments, in many rather concrete ways even. Doesn't the performance of the seemingly discrete archival object start already here, in such an infrastructural extension of archival labor (cf. Birkin 2015)? From the fetishizing of the object remainder, the more interesting route is the backstage of labor and energy needed to sustain the regulated observation of that object. Or simply: every archive, museum, and library is constantly, meticulously, and laboriously maintained. We will return to this

[Figure 1.3.] Image from the *Archive Space* exhibition, curated by Dr. Jane Birkin. Image courtesy of Special Collections, Hartley Library, University of Southampton

question later, in the context of issues of infrastructure as well as obsolete hibernated stocks of technological culture that seem to form the other environmental context of remain(s).

Of course, we know that places of cultural heritage are places of and for objects. This sort of a display-case approach to the past

[Figure 1.4.] Image from the *Archive Space* exhibition, curated by Dr. Jane Birkin. Image courtesy of Special Collections, Hartley Library, University of Southampton.

is how museums were in the first place inaugurated as media environments. To gaze and to admire were particular gestures that performed the space as it was supposed to be performed— as a stage of historical intrigue and also distance. Such were the learned affective attitudes that connected the new techniques of looking from dioramas to shopping arcades and department stores (Henning 2006, 5–36), while also becoming embedded in particular nation-state functions of educational value. As Michelle Henning (2006, 46–52) demonstrates, dioramas were places of education while producing a visual spectacle of social and natural history. The visibility included how time was maintained as if frozen; time was mediated as a photographic snapshot where the visitor is a spectator admiring a scene: to visit an imaginary past as a situation catered before your eyes.

The focus on *places* of cultural heritage—as media environments of display, spectacle, viewing, gazing, and admiring but also as mediated environments of infrastructures and spatial control as well as labor—starts to draw our attention to this particular way of looking at remains. Here the place becomes invested in all the dynamics that enable it. This means considering the *situations, even actioned situations,* in which remains remain, multiply, change form, become rearranged: through an investigation of the material remains, media archaeology and media studies establish a connection not only to practices and spaces of curating and collections but also to methods in contemporary archaeology, in other words, site-specific and spatial situations of encounter of remains of "old" media cultures in ways that are not only an epistemological issue of classifications. It becomes a way to look at the spaces and situations, as well as the extended networks that sustain those containments and act as their constitutive outsides.

As different solutions to the issues of the presencing past, some approaches in media theory have opened up the topic through the idea of the monument. This approach consists of underlining that the remainder of the past is an actual past with us, even if met with the particular situations of the contemporary. The media theoretical work of Wolfgang Ernst is one example of an emphasis on media cultural objects and apparatuses that persist as the monuments in the sense that Michel Foucault's work already laid out. While Foucault's work has at times been branded as the more metaphorical archaeology, it still has been a strong part of the discussions about the materiality of the culture. Not merely the discursive impact but the wider nondiscursive situations, institutions, and conditions are part and parcel of the wider sense of this "archaeological." It also triggers a way to look at contemporary media cultural artifacts as residuals of the past. This is slightly different than considering past artifacts as dead media. Instead, they are still alive even if not always very well. Ernst is keen to emphasize that this materiality is the shared focus of the archaeologist and the media archaeologist. This is both a way to distance media archaeology from history—both as a style of narrative and as a methodology—and to bring it into proximity with the archaeological discourse.

For Ernst, archaeology is an approach that works in many ways in contrast to history. It focuses not on what there was that is resurrected as a narrativized form of remembering or as "the past," or even the trace, but on what is present, at hand, and somehow insisting its proximity upon us. Despite often focusing—and as we will soon see, collecting—so-called old media, the main emphasis is not merely archival but on the epistemological conditions that this sort of an understanding brings about. Ernst (2013, 57) writes,

> "Historic" media objects are radically present when they still function, even if their outside world has vanished. Their "inner world" is still operative. Both classical archaeologists and media archaeologists are fascinated by the hardware of culture, its artifacts—from ancient marbles up to electromechanical engineering products. Both approaches have a *fundamentum in re*: the hard-edged resistance of material objects that undo historical distance simply by being present.

Such an epistemological position that includes a focus on the undoing of the distance for the benefit of proximity comes out clearest in some of the practices and supporting conditions in which the objects are approached. Hence, instead of mere analysis of theoretical concerns, I am interested in the spatial situations of such a proposition as a form of "applied media theory" (O'Gorman 2012) even. Instead of an off-the-self approach to analysis of media, how does one create situations in which objects of media studies become remains and yet an active, reconfigurable, even operational part of the present through sustained, sometimes even speculative collections? Where does it come from; how is it situated? What is the background in which one can start to unfold the idea of proximity and presence, not merely as such a sort of fallacy that Derrida warned about but as a sort of active, dynamic, and material relation that later in this essay will be also elaborated through the notion of speculative collections (Nowviskie 2016). Indeed, as a way to understand the conditions of such theoretical proposition, it is rather important to note the role of the Media Archaeological Fun-

[Figure 1.5.] The Media Archaeological Fundus, an image of the earlier cellar space at Sophienstrasse, Berlin. Courtesy of Media Studies, Humboldt University, Berlin. Image used with permission.

dus and other sites as creative infrastructures for encounters with remains of technological past as archaeological objects. In addition, one should mention the complementary work of the Signal Lab upstairs in the same building in the Media Studies Institute. Both contribute toward spatial situations of remain(s). Let's start with the Fundus, which lies, at least metaphorically, at the bottom.

In Ernst's (2015) words, the founding of the Fundus related to an institutional shift and a reorientation that came with the founding of the chair for media studies. An administrative event was tied up with a spatial event:

> When in 2003 the seminar for Media Studies was found-
> ed at Humboldt University in Berlin, it replaced former
> Theatre Studies. All of the sudden, spaces like the stu-
> dent practicing stage and its relating fund of objects
> for rehearsal were empty. This was the ideal moment
> for the Berlin school of media studies (insisting on the

materialities of communication and epistemic technologies) to claim such rooms under new auspices. The stage became the Media Theatre where technical devices themselves become the protagonist, and the fundus became the space for a collection of requisites of a new kind: media archaeological artefacts.

The legacy in performance and theater was transferred and transposed into a different sort of relationality, which was also tied to certain spatial practices involving objects. The space of the remainder is the stage, the background setting of the remainder of the media archaeological object where students, research, and other activities establish relations to things. But it is not a background as a passive scene but an active milieu which becomes involved in it all. Mary Douglas (1986) once asked in a series of essays not if but how institutions think. We can continue, how do collections think? How do collections and labs and spatial situations make us think?

Distance is one form of organizing institutions—what goes where, and how close to that thing can you come—that is the allowed form of touching and in whose hands the institution allows. Oddly enough, these are questions that become relevant for media theory, too, especially when put into the context of various institutions of memory and its material legacy. As a space of haptic knowledge (acknowledged or not, confirmed or left for the visitor to realize), the Fundus reads against some of the established practices of museums where distance is upheld for the sake of display. Despite Ernst's theoretical ideas paradoxically speaking about the "cool distance" of the analytical gaze, the methodologies are actually embedded in a more embodied way of looking at and touching media. This sort of a tension between cool distances and performative proximities becomes, however, fruitful. Ernst (2015) continues on the concrete (re)sources for such analysis that is the condition of existence of analysis instead of mere consultation of documents:

> For academic media analysis it requires a pool of past media objects which teachers and students are allowed to

operate with, different from the "don't touch" imperative in most museums. The Media Archaeological Fundus is populated with core technological molecules which at first glance look outdated but become a-historical once they are deciphered with media-archaeological eyes, ears and minds. A telegraphy apparatus turns out to be "digital" *avant la lettre,* surpassing the age of so-called "analog" signal media like the classic electric telephone.

Collections come in many guises, and the museum should be seen as only one particular institutional suggestion that pertains to the past. In which ways could the depot, the lab, and the studio become part of staging the remains? One is invited to touch only when in specific, regulated environments, preferably with plastic gloves (see Schneider, this volume), whereas the historical precedents and alternatives open up alternative practices too, for example, the cabinets of curiosity, *Wunderkammern,* were ways to negotiate the morphing relations between the natural and the artificial, as Horst Bredekamp (1995) argued. The showcasing of the machine emerged in specific dynamic spatial practices. Bredekamp emphasizes that these cabinets had a special role in mediating from prescientific to scientific practices (including the laboratory); but they were not merely about logocentric forms of organization, giving form to heterogeneous objects but a more dynamic form of exchange: "Especially since natural objects were mixed with works of art and technology, the historicity of the materials—and not an ahistorical logocentricity of linguistic nomenclature—was conveyed" (110). In some cases, these sites started to become also spaces for experimentation, emphasizing the dynamics of objects. They are not merely things but potentials for triggering other things, events, transformations. I will return to cabinets of curiosity in the final section of this text through a recent exhibition, *Cabinets of Consequence* at University College London (UCL), that stages the remainders of culture in relation to what sorts of imaginaries might emerge from a consideration of the spatiotemporal conditions of collections. The container opens up to its constitutive networks of production.

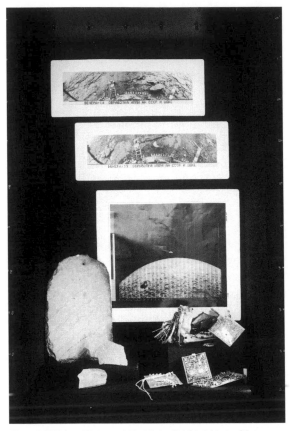

[Figure 1.6.] Helena Hunter and Mark Peter Wright, *Cabinets of Consequence*, Octagon Gallery, University College London, 2016. Photograph by Matt Clayton. Used with permission.

It is important to think of collections and practices of remains, such as the many labs and like, as departing from the ideals of the museum. This could be thought of as complementing the other functions by way of alternative legacies. Darren Wershler picks up on a similar thread when introducing his Montreal-based Residual Media Depot: not quite a lab, not really a museum, but a

research collection that continues the earlier traditions of research
collections in universities. As Wershler puts it, recent media and
humanities institutes have returned to emphasize earlier traditions
of collections that defined much of nineteenth-century university
teaching and research:

> Research and teaching collections preserve a wide range
> of objects, including (but not limited to) scientific instru-
> ments, mineral samples, art objects, chapbooks and
> ephemera, consumer goods, magazines, architectural
> models, taxidermied animals, film, tissue samples, digi-
> tal files, toys and archaeological antiquities. Regardless
> of their role in the establishment of many disciplines,
> the history, structure and function of university collec-
> tions (not-quite libraries, not-quite archives) remain
> under-theorized and poorly understood. (pers. comm.,
> October 5, 2016)

However, in many cases, one calls such places of interaction with
old objects, cultural heritage, and media *laboratories.* For sure, it
is a term usually reserved for scientific practices and preserves
the connotations of big science labs but increasingly over the past
years has been used also in contexts of the humanities (Earhart
2015). This particular, more modest and grassroots-scale sort of
lab activity of shared spaces, hands-on approaches, methodologies
of tinkering and collective "doing it together" spirit, applies also to
the other part of the Institute, complementary to the Fundus: the
Signal Laboratory. As Stefan Höltgen (2016) characterizes especially
the Signal Lab but also by implication the Fundus, they are "technologically 'infected' humanities labs, . . . teaching electronics, programming, and topics of the informatics/computer sciences from
the viewpoint of media theory." The particular idea of a research
collection is strongly present in the way the Signal Lab is thought
of. It is something that stems from a strong enthusiasm for the
media historical object, which could easily be designated as "retro"
or even nostalgic attachment to a past era. But Höltgen wants to
emphasize that this sort of attachment to what remained is not

really merely about nostalgia—or to put it more accurately, nostalgia is at most part of a bigger critical methodology of engagement with technology:

> Nostalgia is a very important "first trigger" for re-using old/dead/vintage hardware and software. But most of those users would withdraw their activities when the feeling of nostalgia disappears. We tell those users that nostalgia isn't really the energy for their engagement because you can't use an "old medium": the moment you turn it on it is totally present/in presence. Even if you use your C64 with its old floppy drive and old games you are playing those games now and you are bringing it to function now. So the term "retro" isn't just a badge for "vintage culture" but a figure of time for the "short cut" between the past and the present. Perhaps nostalgia is the Freudian (un) canny feeling of this short cut—that you are never be able [*sic*] to return to the past but to resume past activities with present knowledge, culture, and technology.

To think in terms of a trigger implies action, performance, embodied relation, engagement, intervention, and hands-on investigation as a mode of operating with the material past that is not merely vintage of a surface. Can the remainder become actioned in this way, which becomes part of the extended support network of research and teaching, too? How is the time of the remainder maintained and relayed?

The various examples, ideas, and explanations that Ernst and Höltgen offer highlight that such spaces as the Fundus and the Signal Lab still have to do with media archaeological pasts, but not as signs of the past that disappeared, a past gone by, a past that remains mystically mute and silent. More accurately, the collections are hybrid sites of learning, theory, and, to some extent, indeed, collecting. But these are not history collections. They stand back in other ways, especially when they enter into the hands of a media archaeological epistemologist. Instead of history, Ernst's way of dealing with the existence of material media technologies is to see them as an epistemological and pedagogical challenge. By placing himself in the theoretical legacy of Foucault, Ernst insists on the importance of understanding these artifacts as monuments: the primacy of the remainder becomes an object in itself instead of a mere index to historical reconstruction. The objects are not props for a writing of a historical narrative but instead are involved in production of theory that is itself executed in a place. Haraway is not mentioned in these discussions but probably should be: no god's-eye view. Theory needs its own place, sometimes a vector. Hence the objects are also anchors, and yet they work less as individual historical fetishes and need to be investigated as part of a series that can be rearranged and reconfigured (Ernst 2013, 44). It is this possibility to rearrange what already seems to exist that becomes both a commentary about the taxonomic remains and the material, even speculative practice.

But as technical media are no object in the Greek vase sort of a way, further methodological considerations are needed; in other words (as Ernst argues), as technical media are not to be judged only by their quality as visual, material objects of surfaces, they are to be approached in operation. The remains of media are not the most interesting thing as an antiquarian appreciation of old things in corners of a museum but as operations that demonstrate in which ways they are media. It is here that the issue of remains starts to operate through the notion of the monument, but a monument that refers to the operationality of the technology. The time-critical and microtemporal operations that define signal-based media become here "the remains" in an interesting turn that at the same time tries to account the signal remains and yet through practices such as situated labs or the Fundus, where the relation to signals can be measured, analyzed, performed. It is also here that the notion of presence becomes complexified. In a paradoxical way, it becomes in some way possible to talk of the remains of the signal, itself a time-critical and, one could say, ephemeral part of electronic culture. Hence the remains are not merely objects or such but can be rather more complex entities that do not merely fall into something tangible.

In other words, to avoid the fallacy that the object bridges a direct connection to the past, we are better off to emphasize the rather processual accounts in this emphasis on the situations, performances, and material signals of the remains. Winthrop-Young (2015) puts it accurately: Ernst's account of microtemporality actually brings into play a different sort of a way of tackling the remains than merely addressing the object of the past and the present in historical time. Instead, the constant emphasis that machines create their own temporal sequences becomes a way to tap into the remainder in an alternative way. Winthrop-Young continues elaborating by way of emphasizing the radical stakes for discussions in history:

> What we are dealing with is the perspective that time may dissolve into a flash of strings and bursts in ways that recall the dissolution of space and matter on the smallest subatomic scale. Time becomes a strange amorphous beast: folded, intersected, and recursively processed; and the media archaeologist emerges as a time whisperer in synch with the alien or untamed—the xeno- or agriochronic—noise of time. (146)

The staging of a performative relation to time becomes actually a way of exploding the notion of presence of remains into a meditation of other times. The situations of stages, performances of encounter of remains, are not merely meant to place an object on its linear historical place but to investigate how it might actually be able to enter into an epistemological playfulness as to what time is, "what counts as time" (Winthrop-Young 2015, 147). Indeed, epistemology becomes understood as a situated practice, as a lab situation, an affective meditation on ontology of time in media culture. How does one become entangled in the contemporary that is itself one key temporal marker that complexifies the notion of present (against which notions of old, new, remains, residuals, could be measured) (see Cox and Lund 2016; cf. Haraway 2016)?

Can the contemporary be arranged and approached as spatial practice? How does it manifest in architecture and as infrastructure? Closer to the vocabulary of design, making, and practice-based encounters with material worlds, we are dealing with the issue of arrangements that range from singular objects to theoretical ideas. How do you arrange such things in space, into a practice, and as techniques that pertain to forms of teaching and research of media? In which ways are practices of making already embedded in a complex negotiation that moves away from too easy coordinates of old, new, obsolescent, emergent? Some of the labs and the Fundus are such spaces of reconfiguration that does not become a work of history but hands-on epistemology. This has its own particular resonance with how critical making has made its own significant entry across many of the discussions in the humanities writ large, hence finding another echo across disciplinary divisions. Matt Ratto (2011, 254) refers to the work of critical making as engaged in "transitional objects—gears, computers, other physical objects—as a way of connecting the sensorimotor 'body knowledge' of a learner to more abstract understandings," an idea he reconstructs from Seymour Papert. Here the abstract understanding can become the temporal horizon that engages with a complex multitemporality; ideas of short-circuiting can become a conceptual lead for engagement with objects of past media cultures, of transitional triggers that sort out the remainder as itself both situated and also vehicle onward.[2]

One can also observe that the issue forks into some key directions. To echo the words above, the relation to the remainder becomes a situated and, one could say, performative practice, even an experience. Even if the main body of Ernst's media theory—and in some ways following some of Kittler's notes about technical media irreducible to the human sensorial—refuses to talk about the emphatic experiential, the Media Archaeological Fundus is exactly such a place where remains are staged in relation to the practices, techniques, and bodies that work there. As part of situations of teaching as well as research excursions, there is an element of staging, performative, hands-on relation in discovering issues of epistemology by way of the dynamic relation. A small example: videos from the Fundus often feature hands. The hands that are operating, pointing, opening up a remain of a thing become partial agents in this play. It's also the hands that are somewhat quietly at the center of what is explained as the difference between the performative and the operative. The hands give way to the technomathematical operation. The operator's hands withdraw, at least in the narrative Ernst (2014) offers (in one of his lectures), while himself, constantly, using his hands:

> Hands, our human hands, actually got more and more off machines by automation. From the anthropological view, the hand as tool has been both the central definition and already an extension of man. Machinic type-writing has differentiated the hands into ten discrete fingers. Finally, the binary code reduces even the decimal fingers to two. What still looks like a playful performative handicraft in reality is already a techno-mathematical operation. While my fingers hack such thoughts in symbolic code on the keyboard of my laptop, the media archaeological distance is aware that most writing is done within the microprocessors themselves, where algorithms reign.

Are the hands the obsolete sort of a remainder? An obsolete human being, an image of something of an antiquated past form of tool making and graspability? Or part of a more complex entanglement where the technomathematical is definitely not operating on the level of the embodied handcrafting human being, and yet we need interfaces through which to engage with that which is beyond reach? How do you engage with the other scales if not through the body as a sort of a threshold—not a celebration of the human body but a mobilization of its possibilities as part of the thresholds, interfaces that move across scales and make the body already something else than it is (see Braidotti and Vermeulen, 2014; see also Schneider, this volume).

Furthermore, as Ernst (2015, 23) himself acknowledges, this is where performance (theory) and contemporary archaeology share some similarities and can engage in an exchange. Here the link to theoretical work in performance studies, not least Rebecca Schneider's writing, becomes clearest: what is the performative dimension that offers a dynamic way to understand the archival and move beyond oppositions of live and documented, live and recorded, to the productive liveness of the archival as an embodied situation. Ernst's acknowledgment of the proximity of some of the questions that are shared between both fields connects to a performative dimension of engaging with the remainder of technoculture. But acknowledging how both performance and archaeology can relate to the media theoretical task, such an agenda of the presence of the past is what demands that we address "questions over how we create relationships with that which remains" (Giannachi, Kay, and Shanks, quoted in Ernst 2015, 23). Not repeating Ernst's words just to reinstate his argument, but using his ideas to trigger a further appreciation of these spatial, embodied, and yet not-merely-human interfaces, one can point out that this is not only a question of personalized relation, such as can become collective events, and facilitated by institutional practices that acknowledge this aspect. In other words, it relates to the question of what sort of spatial practices in media studies and media archaeology can facilitate this engagement and is often answered by the intensive spread of "labs" as the answer to the transformation of the humanities.

Remains start to take another sort of a shape: more pedagogical and more oriented toward making or design, as briefly noted earlier. Hence we are not dealing only with the usual conceptual spatial reference point of the archive, and this is why sorts of attachments start to feature; some of these are borrowed from history of art, some come from history of science, some from histories of collecting, transporting, and storing. It might be, for example, a depot, or perhaps the studio, that becomes a central stage for the remains that start to operate in institutional situations, in different hands, in different settings of epistemological concerns. It starts to connect to issues less of the past than those of design. Labs and studios embody a different attitude and epistemology; despite the proximity between the two, well noted by historians of science and art (Galison and Jones 1999), they incorporate still somewhat a different ontological approach to the remainder, even if we are at the moment witnessing archives and cultural heritage institutions increasingly trying to "reanimate" collections by way of redefining their function as more audience oriented, open and transparent.[3]

Bethany Nowviskie has referred to the idea of "speculative collections" that would actively acknowledge and rework the idea of the historical archive from merely reproducing narratives of power to alternative speculative futures and pasts. In her words:

> Maybe the best way for the digital library community, in particular, to help break the sense of fatalism, inevitability, and disaffection from the historical archive that dominant narratives can provoke is to take seriously the Afrofuturist notion of cultural heritage not as content to be received but technology to be used. How do you position digital collections and digital scholarly projects more plainly not as statements about what was, but as toolsets and resources for what could be? (Nowviskie 2016)

Instead of special collections, Nowviskie's call for speculative collections reminds of the necessity to think of institutions and techniques of cultural memory as implying an active task that demands a stance toward a future too. Nowviskie's way of bringing Afrofuturist ideas in art, theory, popular culture, and black activism to discussions of cultural heritage and memory is particularly enlightening as a way to think beyond just the idea of memory as a sort of sustaining of the contemporary moment. Referring to John Akomfrah's film *Last Angel of History* and the legacy of black music cultures it presents as well as to contemporary forms of projects such as Black Quantum Futurism, Nowviskie utilizes key ideas, such as the archival imaginary and "usable pasts" from those practices. From art projects to community activism, Nowviskie explicates key ideas that could benefit digital libraries and memory institutions in ways that are at the center of *memory becoming activism.* In her words:

Grappling—in terms of selection, arrangement, description, and delivery—with the imaginary, with process, with time as situated kairos rather than impersonal chronos, with users as co-creators: all these things would bring us closer to having digital libraries and archives that permit speculation and maybe not only demonstrate, but help to *realize* greater community agency in the context of shared cultural heritage. And if it must be our collective argument now, that research libraries can no longer purchase and house *truly* far-future-oriented collections, collections full of stuff no-one is asking for at present—well, I'll just point out that imaginary archives likely come cheap and don't take up a lot of space. (Nowviskie 2016; see also Drake 2016 on liberatory archives and Black Lives Matter)

This brings a further angle to the more ontological and technology-focused idea of active operational archives of remains of media culture that is backed up by the work in various media archaeologically tuned labs. The question is not either–or but to ask, what does an active, operational, and multiscalar approach to holdings, remains, and more enable? It is a question of a memory that never just was but always becomes. This becoming is situated in particular spaces of making/thinking but also in particular historical situations that, for example, have relation to issues of race, gender, sexuality, immigration status, and more. Hence the remain(s) become more of an event that summons new relations and potentials than merely a thing to be classified; it expands outside its cabinets, classifications, and index systems to the histories, the archaeological sediments, and the great outdoors from which it comes. This gesture itself is important and is more than just an interesting ontological realization about technical media and liveness.

The switch between activism and art is particularly interesting. The extension of practices of remains from the archive to the lab or the maker space is one way of making sense of what operationality might mean in this context. But also in experimental (media) arts, the idea of the active archive has surfaced. The contemporary art group Constant has mobilized its Active Archives as one way of realizing the importance of infrastructures in cultural memory situations—to approach the remains in and of archives not merely as residual but as potential means also to develop particular technological affordances to support this work.

Michael Murtaugh and Nicolas Maleve's work as part of Constant has produced collaborative projects that extend existing archives into new software supported art projects. This project that was started in 2006 intuitively resonates with Nowviskie's later formulation in many ways and highlights the possibilities of software-based work that is both infrastructural and also artistic. In other words, the developed free software relates to discussions about open standards but also provides a further active platform for new work. Their joint projects with the archive of the Scandinavian Institute of Comparative Vandalism (SISV) (which originates from the work by Asger Jorn with Peter Glob and Werner Jacobsen in 1961) as well as earlier with the pioneering media artist and technologist Erkki Kurenniemi's archive (in Helsinki) produced infrastructurally interesting new solutions to cultural heritage—as well as new artistic work.[4]

Together with theorist Geoff Cox, Maleve and Murtaugh (2015, 125) explain that this work is part of a project to think archives differently; "not to follow standardized archiving procedures of ordering and classifying, but to offer a series of speculations on the specific qualities of the materials by running computer programs." One could speak of providing a new infrastructure for the liveness of the archives—to disperse meanings, to distribute and decentralize the archive as an event instead of a place or a stable thing. Here the particular affordances of software and programming amount to more than "just" a supportive function; history and remains are more than just passive material waiting for a narrativization and amount to dynamic potentials in "techniques to uncover (and compile) aspects of what is not directly apparently in the material— beyond visual and tactile apperception" (126). In the case of their work on the Kurenniemi archive, this amounted to teasing out

themes already part of Kurenniemi's own thinking about embodiment, the posthuman, the generative power of technology and
algorithms, and what to do with the mass of documents Kurenniemi recorded for later generations to use to (re)construct his data
double—a weird sort of a legacy, even a transhumanist fantasy,
that doubles up as recursive speculative life. But it also becomes
a way to think of the archive as an entity that folds into so many
levels, potentials, and scales and to take some of the impulses as
part of a certain forensic drive that defines this active archiving
fever. The archive might come as a whole, but it is unfolded only by
asking, what can the archive do?

An apt example is how Constant approaches the algorithmic support systems and software probes as "conversational agents that
perform forensic operations." This can be said to be about working
with the particular metadata of the holdings, such as images or, for
example, audio material in an archive, but in ways that it becomes
more than just a way to understand the image. It becomes a way
to produce the image anew through various algorithmic procedures (for example, familiar from computer vision techniques
involving face detection, contour detection, color measurement,
and metadata extraction, as they list). Hence their idea of a data
gallery actually goes deeper into the archival object (for example,
an image) as a way to problematize the scale of what is seen as the
remainder:

Imagine a picture.

An horizontal picture 2592 pixels wide and 1944 pixels
high.

The picture was taken on the 06th of November 2004
at 21h56:37. The document set contains 45732 pictures
by Erkki Kurenniemi for the year 2004. Erkki took 223
pictures in 2004 between the hours of 9 and 10pm. Of the
45732 pictures present in the dataset, Erkki took 33712 at
night.

In the folder where this file is located, there are 28
other pictures. They have been taken between 21h56:32

and the next day at 19h21:18. The folder *Harrin bileet* can be seen as a sequence of 21 hours 24 minutes 46 seconds of the life of a man of 63 years 4 months at the date the picture was taken.

It took 1/40th second for the camera to take the picture. The blink of an eye. (Kurenniemi Active Archives-project log, quoted in Cox, Maleve, and Murtaugh 2015, 135)

In a sort of algorithmic version of a Leibnizian universe, the archival image opens to multiple new realities, images, and relations, and relations of relations. It is a further way to open up what was discussed earlier in terms of the media archaeological impulse of operationality that for example Ernst proposes, and the particular situated nature of the remains. Such projects offer different angles for the move from archives of remains that are for cataloging and such ordered systems of indexing to the forensic, speculative, activist, and hence also more distributed situations and techniques. In the next section, I want, however, to problematize this aspect of the remains by way of alternative situations of the remain where some point to urban remains that are not museum objects, some point to the remainders of production, and some point to the remainders where the taxonomic restrictions unleash imaginary potentials of speculative collections as an art practice. This again folds back as part of the earlier connections to the performative dimensions of the remains even if continuously in this text discussed in contexts of media and technology.

All That Remains Melts into Its Outside

Media archaeological investigations into old, obsolete, recurring, and forgotten media cultures seem often focused on things. By this I mean that despite some significant differences, many of the approaches establish their frame of reference around a particular media technology, or a discursive field of media (including practices and techniques). But how to move from a materiality of objects to a materiality of environments—environments of memory and their operational existence (perhaps echoing Schneider's use of the term, as slough media)? As Giuliana Bruno (2016) argues, discussing materiality of archives as places of memory, "materiality is, in fact, a gray zone, and a place of complex mnemonic relations. It is not a question of materials themselves or a matter of 'thingness' per se but rather concerns the substance of material relations and connections and how they are configured on the surface of different media." Such surfaces of media extend much outside the thing itself and to the constitutive networks that define the planetary level of material media remains. This outside is of particular political and material importance.

Besides many implications for the utterly peculiar and interesting question as to what sort of materialities have their own time and, as such, matter, it also begs the question, how about wider scales of infrastructure, of urban and planetary scales, of rural networks and abandoned sites that are architectural remains? The discourse in disciplines of history on locations of memory can be taken into rather concrete sites of abandoned and obsolete remains that are still something to account for when it comes to discussions of material remains. One speaks of storage *space,* which, however, is not merely a site of materials but often more akin to "a place of complex mnemonic relations" (Bruno 2016), in the sense that the cabinets of curiosities are but also for example teaching and research collections from (media) depots to labs.

Speaking of spaces and architectures, one obviously can point to the bunker archaeology that already had a significant effect in understanding the continuations of the architectures of World War II to the Cold War and on to contemporary art and media theory (Virilio 1994). But besides the wars that are key sites for memorials, and key sites of reference for many media theorists, one might add, we can also point to the work in urban ecology and related disciplines that looks at remains of the city as a site of industrial scrap: metals and other materials, residues of chemistry and possibly reusable things. This insight is important for rather practical

[Figure 1.7.] Image from the *Archive Space* exhibition, curated by Dr. Jane Birkin. Image courtesy of Special Collections, Hartley Library, University of Southampton.

ends: to discuss possible toxic legacies of technological culture and to investigate possibilities of reuse of materials, for example, copper that remains of the wired city. What an archaeological discovery of a past media culture! Björn Wallsten explains this aspect in more detail in his research on urban mining and hibernating infrastructures, exposing the situated nature of remains on a different scale, not merely as a thing but as a site. Wallsten's way of narrating the longer-term understanding of the city as a sedimented layer of mines that can be defined both by the inverted mines of buildings like skyscrapers (Brechin 1999; Wallsten 2013, 1) and less glamorous places of residue, such as landfills, is something that does not intuitively fit in the usual framework of media and technology studies but importantly expands the media archaeological agenda. The remains of technological culture are not just things of a media historical collection value that include (rare or not) instruments of recording, transmitting, receiving, calculating, and other things that reside in museums, labs, collections, and other sites of staged obsolescence. But they can be things out there, too: broken systems, infrastructural remains, landfills and

travels of waste from synthetic to metallic. Referring to Jane Jacobs,
Wallsten (2013) talks of the urban sediments, cities, as the mines of
the future, but he also introduces another interesting concept that
can be interfaced with our media-focused concerns. *Hibernating
stocks* hence refers to "entities with material content that has been
removed from service but has not yet entered the waste sector" (2),
which can include electronic equipment lying around but also the
"abandoned parts" of "old industrial cities" that contain "significant
amounts of cables and pipes that remain under the streetscape
after having been taken out of use" (3).

Besides the practical value in investigating cities as multiple layers
of useful materials that preserve this usefulness also after their
primary use-value, it also reminds of the important techniques and
practices that keep technological culture running at all. Themes of
repair and maintenance (see, e.g., Graham and Thrift 2007) return
again, just like they were raised in Nowviskie's call for speculative
collections. Here the remains are not merely the long trail of past
events that sediment as the (dysfunctional) residual. The remains
are the longer network and condition of existence of the various
activities that make anything work in the first place. In other words,
both as labor and as infrastructure, repair and maintenance
transport us to the remainder of a sort of a different kind and
of a different location not so easily discoverable at first sight in
organized official sites of memory and (re)collection.

As many wonderful scholars working on infrastructure point out,
the materiality of technical media expands into distributed networks, locations, and situations. Shannon Mattern (2015) recounts
that an interest in making urban and rural infrastructures visible is
complementing the picture of the material deep times of remains
that we have at hand; media history becomes architectural history;
media objects, even operationality, become questions of infrastructure, and the question of "remains" becomes even more difficult,
as it cannot be pinpointed as one solitary thing. Urban communication networks, to paraphrase Mattern, never return merely
to issues of media as tangible objects at hand, and definitely not

merely to singular devices only (xi). What's there more then? Wallsten's outline is useful in this regard even if coming from a different
disciplinary background. And similarly, the focus on infrastructure
opens new temporal and spatial ways of understanding what is and
what was and what persists, and where it does all of this.

From signals to cables, electricity grids to data center architecture
and more (see Parks and Starosielski 2015; Starosielski 2015),
there is a wider ecology of remains that opens up in at least two
directions. On one hand, this is material for the media archaeologist of infrastructures. These examples are extensions of the
infrastructure tours that map the wider spatial distribution of
media in surprising locations (Mattern 2013). Media remains are
not merely things for cabinets and museums, collections, and such
but also places and spaces of encounters of media of scale that go
beyond a thing for the hand or the eyes. Infrastructural tourism
tours are one type of evidence of site-specific psychogeographies
of mapping media spots—not merely hot spots but also cold spots
(cf. Wallsten 2013), as research in industrial ecology calls them;
places and material infrastructures of copper, cables, wires, and
more, falling out of use.

On the other hand, besides solitary (media archaeological)
laboratory objects, this raises the question, what are the methodologies that facilitate this analytical, critical, but also creative (art
and design) work addressing the wider infrastructures that remain
as remnants of technological culture? There are wide-reaching
implications in this realization about sites and networks of media
archaeological remains of cities, of technological pasts. As Mattern
(2013) narrates, "quoting Gregory Bateson, Star and Bowker suggest that an infrastructure is a 'relationship or an infinite regress of
relationships.' Never a 'thing.'" Let's continue this trail of thoughts
and suggest that what remain(s) is never a thing but an infinite
regress of relationships, both in time and also in scattered spaces.
We can again cite interesting examples of projects that engage with
this dispersion. Ingrid Burrington's (2016) *Networks of New York* is a
useful and intuitive guide to how to see the internet as an infra-

structural part of urbanism, and it is a way to start appreciating how it abstracts from the concrete to the various links to surveillance and other institutional networks. Site-specific investigations tours and mapping as collective activity start to unfold a different environmental relation to the actual sites and the remainders of technological infrastructure (see, again, Mattern 2013).

Such mapping, expeditions, and collective work can also be performative: remain unfolds in time and across multiple geographies. It comes out through the methodological structure of the expedition that starts to unfold what the remainder of technological production also might be. Designers and studios, such as Liam Young and Kate Davies's Unknown Fields Division, address the wider infrastructural question through annual design research expeditions to the peripheries of infrastructures of technology; container ship traffic, e-waste in Mongolia, lithium mining in Bolivia, the rural landscapes that are essential as the planetary-scale "conveyor belt" of technological, remain as an issue also for the broader context of critical design.

[Figure 1.8.] Unknown Fields Division, Rare Earthenware. Image by Toby Smith. Used with permission.

38   One of their recent years' major projects *Rare Earthenware* (2015)
focused on the multiple material situations in which electronic
culture happens through a sort of odd object, a radioactive toxic
Ming vase replica. The trip itself was an investigation into the
systems of the logistics and production of electronics starting from
the remainder of mineral processing in Baotou, located in Inner
Mongolia: the toxic sludge provided the radioactive material for the
object itself—a mock Ming vase, but made of "a cocktail of acids,
heavy metals, carcinogens and radioactive material—including
thorium and uranium—used to process the seventeen most sought
after minerals in the world, known as rare earths" (Unknown Fields
Division 2016, 376). The design of such a vase from the tailings is
both a commentary on what it takes to construct electronic culture
and technology and also a sort of odd cultural heritage object.
Here the museum and exhibition object are turned inside out: the
museum houses the e-waste trail and toxicity that produce the
contemporary world instead of the usual remainder of media technological past. The mock Ming vase ended up as part of the Victoria
and Albert Museum's *Luxury* exhibition in London in 2015, but also
indicating this other sort of unfolding of what remains. What if
nothing else remained but the toxicity?[5] What does any object that
ends up in the contained space of cultural heritage bring with it?

Rare Earthenware is one of the more visible and large scale of the
projects. But it is surrounded by other, as engaging ones that are
implicitly important for our topic of the remain(der) too. What
does the museum contain and, while containing it, rely on? What
forms of transport and extraction are part of the production of
situations of memory? The colonial backbone of the museum
institution is one version of this story, but the other, a spatially
scattered planetary set, is about the contemporary infrastructures.
What constitutes the materiality of contemporary object and
image culture, and what are the leftovers and remains of those
objects as they pertain to questions of the production of historical
value? This question envelops the object, and its institution, in the
infrastructural vastness scattered across locations of production
and transport.

[Figure 1.9.] Unknown Fields Division, *Rare Earthenware*. A rare earth refinery. Image by Toby Smith. Used with permission.

A further example will link up spatial practices (this time curating) and the categorization of remains and their afterlives. The exhibition *Cabinets of Consequence* (2016),[6] by artists Helena Hunter and Mark Peter Wright, was open until May 2017 at the UCL. The exhibition picked up on the practice of cabinets of curiosities (mentioned earlier in this essay, too) as one particular form of display. Besides a visual display and using space as an interface to collections, the artist-curators also explain it as a logic of juxtaposition that provides a curatorial line relating to the heterogeneous collections of the elite university. Display became seen as a portal, an interface, as well as itself a productive disjuncture of histories of colonial collections and their contexts in contemporary exhibition space. Display is also a form of containment that extracts the longer legacies of objects and their relations, the cascading regress of relationships; besides awareness of the colonial legacy, this provided an opportunity to put the objects into what they call "relational dialogues with ecology, infrastructures and media through the various powers that govern, claim and enact upon them." The Anthropocene unfolds as a story of multiple points in colonial networks, knowledge, and a contemporary focus on multidisciplinary mediated knowledge about the environmental damage on a planetary scale. And it also unfolds as a story of forms of knowledge, display, and control. The repositioning of artifacts from separate museums and collections at University College London, including the Grant Museum of Zoology, Geology Collections, the Petrie Museum, UCL Art Museum, and pathology and bio-anthropology collections, worked to defy existing disciplinary categorizations and to see natural history as part of "a current context of environmental change, techno-scientific acceleration, social-political instability and postnatural histories" (Hunter and Wright, pers. comm., December 20, 2016).

The *Cabinets of Consequence* came in four different types (agriculture–animals, energies–resources, media–natures, and afterlives–extinction) that included four to five clusters of objects and materials. What ensued was actually a strong sense of impossibility of containment as well as the leaks in classifications that are part of the conditions of production of knowledge. Classification always fails, even if it is constantly productive of habits of perceiving the world.

Hunter and Wright (2016) explained to me one particular cabinet relevant to the topic of remain(s). The Afterlives-Extinctions cabinet included the following examples:

- Debris from Cluster 1, crashed European Space Agency Mission, Mullard Space Science Laboratory, UCL
- Photograph of Venus' Surface by Venera 13 and 14 Lander (1982), NASA Regional Planetary Image Facility Collections
- Photograph of Earth from the Moon taken by the U.S. Lunar Orbiter 1 (1966), NASA Regional Planetary Image Facility Collections
- Fossilised flow markings show an excess of water soon after deposition. UCL Geology Collections/Department of Earth Sciences, SS1/37
- Trace fossils of the movement of water show a time and

[Figure 1.10.] Helena Hunter and Mark Peter Wright, *Cabinets of Consequence,* Octagon Gallery, University College London, 2016. Photograph by Matt Clayton. Used with permission.

place where water once flowed. Ripple Marks, Stonesfield Slate, UCL Geology Collections/Department of Earth Sciences, 551/28

• Body shard from a pottery vessel bearing the phrase "Hymn to the Nile Flood" in hieratic (cursive hieroglyphs) from the Ramesseum

The combinations trigger imaginaries and narratives that escape much outside the taxonomic confines. They are, however, intuitively bound into a series—something one might recognize under the broad, and also contested, term *Anthropocene*—that speaks of the cultural impact of technical imaging, technological junk, geology and fossils, natural elements like water, and cultural markers that are inscribed across these materials. Ideas of technological failure combine with the particular epistemologies (machine vision and processing, sensors on satellites, etc.) that technologies enable to function as media. Temporal speculations connect on a planetary scale. Collections become sites around which the wider infrastructures of their own production—both taxonomic and material—are put into question. Needless to say, one particularly interesting option is to relate this with Nowviskie's idea of speculative collection: what is this pointing toward? Where is it situated, of what histories does it speak, but also, what worlds does it enable to bring forth?

John Akomfrah and Trevor Mathison's *All That Is Solid* melts into a speculative sense of memory involving both imaginary pasts and speculative futures. After the discussion in this essay, including different artistic and curatorial contexts and theoretical ideas, one is tempted to rephrase the words from the Akomfrah and Mathison film that had more to do with materialities such as the fog, the voice, and the ephemeral. All that was organized melts in a speculative collection. All that remains triggers a particular future. All that remains is performed, over again in variation, as events, across multiple relays that include spaces, practices, techniques, and infrastructures. All that remains has its own duration that can be teased out also in artistic practice and design expeditions. All that remains.

Akomfrah and Mathison's film is still a fitting reference point in many ways to many art and curatorial practices that play with remainders of taxonomic classification as well as with remains of material nature. The livelihood of the technological object expands

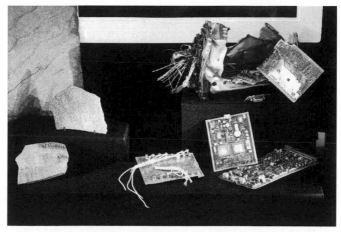

[Figure 1.11.] Helena Hunter and Mark Peter Wright, *Cabinets of Consequence,* Octagon Gallery, University College London, 2016. Photograph by Matt Clayton. Used with permission.

from the operational device to operational infrastructures as well as their own particular tailings. It is of a different scale for a remain that is more than an object and becomes a liveness of multiple afterlives. All *that* remains.

Notes

A warm thank-you to the anonymous reviewer as well as the many people who have read and commented on drafts of this text, including Jane Birkin, Shannon Mattern, Helena Hunter, Mark Wright, Darren Wershler, and Lori Emerson.

1   Thank you to Shannon Mattern for pointing out this context in Stoler's book and how to think such remainders in relation to the colonial production of archival power.

2   Ernst (2016) articulates the relation of hacking and critical making to media archaeology as follows: "Hacking and circuit-bending is a form of media-political criticism, of an economy and artistic experimentation which mostly takes place outside the Humanities departments of academic universities. But when coupled to media studies, the focus of interest is a different one: to reveal and verbally make explicit the knowledge which is implicit in technologies (both in the material and the mathematical sense). Media archaeology as academic

practice is applied epistemology: it does not leave technological expertise to engineering and computing sciences alone but learns and teaches how to create sparks of knowledge from objects in order to translate this into discourse."

3   Thank you to Shannon Mattern for this point.

4   There is obviously a longer history of art practices dealing with the archive. A good starting point for more reading about this link is Sven Spieker's (2008) *The Big Archive: Art from Bureaucracy.*

5   Hence, for example, another art project—*Plastic Imaginaries* (2016) by Kristina Lindström and Åsa Ståhl—includes both workshopping and education toward practical ends of composting and ragpicking and the imaginary projections of plastic futures, where the overabundance of trash turns into a necessity. To quote from their "field guide" in ways that project plastic futures as part of practices and even aesthetics of near-future everydayness, the *plastiglomerate* (a neologism referring to the new natural historical samples made of stones and plastic) is the central figure of this imaginary: "Their windowsill is full of plastiglomerates that the ragpicker has deemed 'beauties.' Sometimes the discrete objects and products can be deciphered, sometimes how the objects fit into old forms of life can be imagined. What plastiglomerates have in common is that due to wasting, currents, weathering, pressure and fires they've become something new; a hybrid matter of stones and plastics and corals and sand and more. Their basement is full of cubes of melted plastics. Like the plastiglomerates, previous objects and practices can only be imagined. Plastic forks, fishing nets, plastic bottles—all kinds of things have merged and become plastic reservoirs. Since newly produced plastics has become scarce, the government has suggested that each household have a 3D printer and at least 1 m3 of plastics at home for emergencies. The recovered plastic is often used to make everyday use objects such as covers for mobile phones and various spare parts to enable repair of domestic technologies" (Lindström and Ståhl 2016, 10). On the natural history of electronics, see Gabrys (2013).

6   https://www.matterlurgy.net/cabinets-of-consequence/.

References

Birkin, Jane. 2015. "Art, Work and Archives: Performativity and Techniques of Production." *Archive Journal,* no. 5. http://www.archivejournal.net/issue/5/archives-remixed/art-work-and-archives/.

Braidotti, Rosi, and Timotheus Vermeulen. 2014. "Borrowed Energy." *Frieze,* August 12.

Brechin, Gray. 1999. *Imperial San Francisco: Urban Power, Earthly Ruin.* Berkeley: University of California Press.

Bredekamp, Horst. 1995. *The Lure of Antiquity and the Cult of the Machine: The Kunstkammer and the Evolution of Nature, Art and Technology.* Translated by Allison Brown. Princeton, N.J.: Markus Wiener.

Bruno, Giuliana. 2016. "Storage Space." *E-Flux,* Istanbul Design Biennial section Superhumanity. November. http://www.e-flux.com/architecture/superhumanity/68650/storage-space/.

Burrington, Ingrid. 2016. *Networks of New York: An Illustrated Field Guide to Urban Internet Infrastructure.* New York: Melville House.

Cox, Geoff, and Jacob Lund. 2016. *The Contemporary Condition: Introductory Thoughts on Contemporaneity and Contemporary Art.* Berlin: Sternberg Press.

Cox, Geoff, Nicolas Maleve, and Michael Murtaugh. 2015. "Archiving the Databody: Human and Nonhuman Agency in the Documents of Erkki Kurenniemi." In *Writing and Unwriting (Media) Art History: Erkki Kurenniemi in 2048,* edited by J. Krysa and J. Parikka, 125–41. Cambridge, Mass.: MIT Press.

Cramer, Florian. 2013. *Anti-media: Ephemera on Speculative Arts.* Rotterdam: nai010/ Willem de Kooning Academie and Institute of Network Culture.

Crary, Jonathan. 1999. *Suspensions of Perception: Attention, Spectacle, and Modern Culture.* Cambridge, Mass.: MIT Press.

Derrida, Jacques. 1995. *Archival Fever: A Freudian Impression.* Translated by Eric Prenowitz. Chicago: University of Chicago Press.

Derrida, Jacques. 2005. *Paper Machine.* Translated by Rachel Bowlby. Stanford, Calif.: Stanford University Press.

Douglas, Mary. 1986. *How Institutions Think.* Syracuse, N.Y.: Syracuse University Press.

Drake, J. M. 2016. "Liberatory Archives: Towards Belonging and Believing." October 26. https://medium.com/on-archivy/liberatory-archives-towards-belonging-and -believing-part-2-6f56c754eb17#.n797x9fcq.

Earhart, Amy. 2015. "The Digital Humanities as a Laboratory." In *Humanities and the Digital,* edited by David Theo Goldberg and Patrik Svensson, 391–400. Cambridge, Mass.: MIT Press.

Ebeling, Knut. 2007. "Die Asche des Archivs." In *Das Archiv brennt,* edited by G. Didi-Huberman and K. Ebeling, 33–183. Berlin: Kadmos.

Ebeling, Knut, and S. Günzel, eds. 2009. *Archivologie: Theorien des Archivs in Philosophie, Medien und Künsten.* Berlin: Kadmos.

Eichhorn, Kate. 2013. *The Archival Turn in Feminisms: Outrage in Order.* Philadelphia: Temple University Press.

Elsaesser, Thomas. 2011. "Freud and the Technical Media: The Enduring Magic of the Wunderblock." In *Media Archaeology: Approaches, Applications, and Implications,* edited by Erkki Huhtamo and Jussi Parikka, 95–115. Berkeley: University of California Press.

Elsaesser, Thomas. 2016. *Film History as Media Archaeology.* Amsterdam: Amsterdam University Press.

Ernst, Wolfgang. 2013. *Digital Memory and the Archive.* Edited with an introduction by Jussi Parikka. Minneapolis: University of Minnesota Press.

Ernst, Wolfgang. 2014. "Digital Media Archaeology: Archive, Museum, Sonicity." Talk given at CCA, Montreal, September 25. https://www.youtube.com/watch?v=f_ GsDqKuOF8.

Ernst, Wolfgang. 2015. "Media Archaeology-as-Such: Occasional Thoughts on (Mes-) alliances with Archaeologies Proper." *Journal of Contemporary Archaeology* 2, no. 1: 15–23.

Ernst, Wolfgang. 2016. "An Interview with Wolfgang Ernst." What Is a Media Lab Project. http://whatisamedialab.com/2016/08/22/an-interview-with-wolfgang-ernst/.

Gabrys, Jennifer. 2013. *Digital Rubbish: Natural History of Electronics.* Ann Arbor: University of Michigan Press.

Galison, Peter, and Caroline Jones. 1999. "Factory, Laboratory, Studio: Dispersing Sites of Production." In *The Architecture of Science,* edited by Peter Galison and E. Thompson, 497–540. Cambridge, Mass.: MIT Press.

Graham, Stephen, and Nigel Thrift. 2007. "Out of Order: Understanding Repair and Maintenance." *Theory, Culture, and Society* 24, no. 3: 1–25.

Haraway, D. J. 2016. *Staying with the Trouble: Making Kin in the Chthulucene.* Durham, N.C.: Duke University Press.

Henning, Michelle. 2006. *Museums, Media and Cultural Theory.* Maidenhead, U.K.: Open University Press.

Höltgen, Stefan. 2016. "An Interview with Stefan Höltgen of the Signal Lab." http://whatisamedialab.com/2016/08/29/an-interview-with-stefan-holtgen-of-the-signal-lab/.

Krajewski, Markus. 2001. "Was zu beweisen war." *Frankfurter Allgemeine Zeitung,* April 12.

Krajewski, Markus. 2014. *World Projects: Global Information before World War I.* Translated by Charles Marcrum II. Minneapolis: University of Minnesota Press.

Lindström, Kristina, and Åsa Ståhl. 2016. *Plastic Imaginaries.* Field Guide. Malmö.

Mattern, Shannon. 2013. "Infrastructural Tourism." *Places,* July. https://placesjournal.org/article/infrastructural-tourism/.

Mattern, Shannon. 2015. *Deep Mapping the Media City.* Minneapolis: University of Minnesota Press.

Mattern, Shannon. 2016. "Cloud and Field." *Spaces,* August. https://placesjournal.org/article/cloud-and-field/.

Nowviskie, Bethany. 2016. *Speculative Collections* (blog). October 27. http://nowviskie.org/2016/speculative-collections/.

O'Gorman, Marcel. 2012. "Broken Tools and Misfit Toys: Adventures in Applied Media Theory." *Canadian Journal of Communication* 37: 27–42.

Parks, Lisa. 2007. "Falling Apart: Electronics Salvaging and the Global Media Economy." In *Residual Media,* edited by Charles Acland, 32–47. Minneapolis: University of Minnesota Press.

Parks, Lisa, and Nicole Starosielski, eds. 2015. *Signal Traffic: Critical Studies of Media Infrastructures.* Urbana: University of Illinois Press.

Ratto, Matt. 2011. "Critical Making: Conceptual and Material Studies in Technology and Social Life." *Information Society* 27: 252–60.

Schneider, Rebecca. 2011. *Performing Remains: Art and War in Times of Theatrical Reenactment.* London: Routledge.

Sobchak, Vivian. 2011. "Afterword: Media Archaeology and Re-presencing the Past." In *Media Archaeology: Approaches, Applications, and Implications,* edited by Erkki Huhtamo and Jussi Parikka, 323–33. Berkeley: University of California Press.

Spieker, Sven. 2008. *The Big Archive: Art from Bureaucracy.* Cambridge, Mass.: MIT Press.

Stoler, Ann. 2009. *Along the Archival Grain: Epistemic Anxieties and Colonial Common Sense.* Princeton, N.J.: Princeton University Press.

Starosielski, Nicole. 2015. *The Undersea Network.* Durham, N.C.: Duke University Press.

Strauven, Wanda. 2011. "The Observer's Dilemma: To Touch or Not to Touch." In *Media Archaeology: Approaches, Applications and Implications,* edited by Erkki Huhtamo and Jussi Parikka, 148–63. Berkeley: University of California Press.

Virilio, Paul. 1994. *Bunker Archaeology.* Translated by George Collins. New York: Princeton Architectural Press.

Wallsten, Björn. 2013. *"Underneath Norrköping An Urban Mine of Hibernating Infrastructure."* Linköping Studies in Science and Technology Licentiate Thesis No. 1617.

Winthrop-Young, Geoffrey. 2015. "Hemerochronia, or, Take a Walk on the Wild Side of Time: Sideline Snippets on Media Archaeology."

[2]

Slough Media

Rebecca Schneider

Resplendent on the face of a small disk made of bone is the unmistakable visage of a human person—an actor—wearing a theatrical mask. Turned in profile, the mask and the masked actor we partially see behind it look off to the side. Through the classical downturn of the tragic mask's large and open mouth, a small, boney tongue still flickers. In fact, like a tiny flying saucer or enterprising starship, this bit of flotsam of the Roman Empire, having picked up detritus of reference from Greece, has ridden Western history's linear-time machine all the way through its Dark Ages, its Renaissance, its Enlightenment and industrializations, across the sprawling Anthropocene, to meet us here in its future, in our mutual "now."

Seen as a photographic image on a computer screen or reproduced in the pages of a book you may be holding in your hands, the small circle of bone—the disk itself—might seem to gaze out at you, even as the little masked face on its face looks off to your left. If you were to hold the disk itself in your hand, as I have done, the double visage of mask and face would become palpable as the wee face lifts off the bone background, sensible to the digitus touch. Whether apprehended by sight or by touch, the small mask on the bone face is full of affect and appears both distracted and alarmed, as if trying to call attention to some tragedy just out of our view or just beyond our reach. Trying to call attention to something else— something other than itself and something out of reach—

[Figure 2.1]. Roman *Gaming Piece,* first century to second century CE. Photograph by Erik Gould. Courtesy of the Museum of Art, Rhode Island School of Design, Providence.

the face of the mask on the face of an actor on the face of a bit of bone looks toward a space off, gesturing toward another scene. Look!

This call to our attention happens through the medium of a mask. The would-be face beneath the mask, signaled here by the back of an actor's head, wields the mask as medium. We cannot see the actor's face, and indeed it is not there. The not-thereness, or otherwhereness, of actors' faces is something that might be said to occur even when actors go unmasked, enacting, as they often do, faces that are not their own. In cinema and other media arts, the face of an actor is not there either, of course, but "preserved" or otherwise mimicked by light or pixels that present themselves, masklike, for dissemination. An originating face is not there, just as, in this bit of bone, the actor's face is not there. Or, as operations of two-facedness might imply, the "face" is there *and* not there at once as one thing (a face) passes for another thing (a face).

As the bit of bone suggests, "the actor" in (your) hand is made to pass. That is, just as actors are mediums of passage, so too are coins, tokens, *tesserae,* or gaming disks. Passing can occur hand to hand, or stage to stage, or screen to screen. And two-facedness explodes, in this way, into many. In the case of this particular bone bit, what we have on the face of the disk is a face upon a face (or, if you prefer, a face beneath a face). A face brokered by a face. Neither face is "really there" but serves to mask their conjoined absence while calling attention to other scenes, coming or going in the space off. Another way to say this is that we have a medium within a medium, in which one medium (the mask) creates the illusion of a user (the mask-wearing actor) calling attention to a space off for a third set of users (you and I and *n*th number of others) who can only encounter the fact that, even with the bit of bone in our very hands, we are absent from the scene the mask virtually cries out for "us" to heed.

Oh, no! the tiny actor's mask seems to call out. *Something's coming!* Or perhaps something is going. Even if that something is coming or going *again,* the experience is brokered *as if* anew.[1] In the iterative play–replay nature of media (theater, photography, film, video, digital arts, as well as gestic techniques of the body), the call or cry circulates, hand to hand, screen to screen, eye to eye, device to device, mouth to mouth. The body that takes the bone disk in hand, extends the medium of the coin and passes it along. The cry circulates. *Oh, no! Look!* The bit of bone beckons (again) toward something *just beyond grasp,* even when held in hand. Out of hand, even while passed hand to hand.[2]

If the Latin word *medium* lies at the root of the word *media,* and if one root meaning of *medium* is "intermediary," then this ancient little disk is surely rendering "media" explicit on its very face. Thousands of years in advance of what we take to be the ever-changing landscape of modern media proper, with its link to "the masses" and endemic thrall to "the new," the reader might reasonably remind me that this bone is not exactly new media and never could have been. It long predates new media's habitual reconstitution through crisis at what Wendy Chun (2016b, 1) calls the "bleeding edge of obsolescence." And yet, the face within the face on the bone seems to be brokering an experience of oncoming–outgoing crisis, the stuff, outmoded or not, of the tragedy it peddles.[3] Next to *crisis,* the keyword here is *brokering,* for arguably, brokering is what media do. In the words of W. J. T. Mitchell and Mark B. N. Hansen (2010, vii), media as intervening substances "broker the giving of space and time within which concrete experience becomes possible" and thus "make knowledge possible in a given historical moment." But surely, if the medium of the bone disk is still brokering experience, still calling out in some way to a space off, and conjuring crisis always just beyond grasp, surely its "given historical moment" is long past?

The given historical moment of this bone disk is the Roman Empire, somewhere in the belly of the first century BCE. As such, this coinlike handheld device cannot touch today's bleeding edge of crisis-chasing media. Today, handheld devices take the shape of cell phones that can call up the digital likeness of this boney bit on their screenal faces in an instant. Today, passing hand to hand is more often passing device-in-hand to device-in-hand. Acknowledging this, can this outmoded "coin" still be considered a medium brokering an *ongoing* scene? For surely, doesn't the disk itself scream only of its own obsolescence? And yet, we might still ask, is the time of its cry ("Something's coming!") *only* past? Or, put another way, to what degree is it the past, perhaps even obsolescence, that is always the "something's coming" brokered by media, new and otherwise?[4]

In this essay, I will ask several questions pertaining to media remains that follow in the wake of this minor, obsolete, and two-faced bit of detritus. Collectible and moderately precious as it may be to antiquarians and historians of ancient Rome, it would seem at first to have little to do with either new media or live performance (performance being my own area of expertise). The word *media* has more conventionally belonged to industrialized modernity—so this ancient bone bit would hardly register as player. But media archaeologists have been challenging the boundaries of media studies to explore media in "deep time" that

can account not only for the flash of contemporary instantaneity
but also for vast stretches of geological time that compose the materiality of media objects. The back cover of Jussi Parikka's (2015)
A Geology of Media, for example, proclaims that media history is
"millions, even billions of year old." Charting the material substrate
particles of media, the bits of mineral and energy that hail from
the "literal deep times and deep places of media in mines" (5),
Parikka reads media, and the matter of which they are recomposed, as part of the broader extraction machine of capitalism. He
cites Benjamin Bratton to remind us that "we carry small pieces
of Africa in our pockets," referring to the role of coltan extracted
from the earth by human and nonhuman laborers in African
mines to take up mobile dwelling in digital media technologies
such as handheld phones. As such, Parikka tells us, geology is
deterritorialized and circulates in flows that *carry along with it*
the histories of extraction, of "social and technical relations and
environmental and ecological realities" (46). Instead of seeing
technology, with McLuhan, as only "extensions of Man," with
humans precariously balanced atop some animacy hierarchy high
above the lowly matter we deploy to extend us, Parikka asks us
to remember that technology is "aggregated and made of the raw
materials of the earth." He mines Donna Haraway on relationality,
to point up the complex entanglement of what he calls "mediana-
ture," a formulation he riffs from Haraway's "natureculture" (13).
Here's Haraway:

> None of the partners pre-exist the relating, and the re-
> lating is never done once and for all. Historical specificity
> and content mutability rule all the way down, into nature
> and culture, into natureculture. (Haraway 2003, 12)

To realign media away from the "new" toward a lineage of a billion
years—to break it "all the way down"—is in part to contradict the
thrall to the newness of technology that has limited our abilities
to account for the depth entanglement of media with earth pro-
cesses, and particularly with the environmental consequences of
the obsolescence machine that modernity's thrall to newness has

spawned. Obsolescence, and the piles of waste in its wake that fill our oceans, our landfills, our atmosphere, is actually a synonym for "new" and a *product* of technologies and bodies. As such, it unsettles our habit of aligning technology with progress. When we acknowledge that obsolescence is a project of the new, the binarized distinction between new and old in thinking about "new media" is exposed as complicatedly corelational. This is something we might have gathered from the Frankfurt School, thinking, for example, of Walter Benjamin's reading of Paul Klee's "Angel of Progress" blown backward by an increasing mountain of trash (see Benjamin 1969, 255–56). But as "old" and oft repeated as this citation may be, stepping aside from the thrall to the new has significant consequences for how we think about the twin ruses of newness and obsolescence in operations of encounter we think of as mediated by technology.

If Parikka and his associates turn to mineral and chemical matter as geologic remains of media, dating media to prehistory, might we also head to the ancient and prehistorical to think again of biomatter, and specifically the *performance* remains of media? For me, this proposition has meant exploring again what so many have explored before: the in-handedness of media. Thinking about flesh and bone as participant in media events clearly makes the so-called live biobody part and parcel of many mediatic encounters.[5] If we consider the live body to be part of some (if not all) mediatic events, this could lead us to thinking of biomatter as media components. But if we also then think, with Parikka, of the bodies of "underpaid laborers in mines or in high-paid entertainment device component factories" (14), are we thinking of biocomponents in broader cross-temporal scenes of media making? This is to consider something like the hand or eye as mediatic when devices pass hand to hand, or eye to eye, even as bodies are scanned for/as information in mediascapes such as airports, city streets, and living rooms. Given that the living biobody is nothing new (and often has been hailed as becoming-obsolete), then the live body too may be a prehistoric component piece of media, remaining and ongoing,

much like the billion-year-old mineral components Parikka hails for
their deep-time participation.[6]

Let's think about this further with the help of an analogy. Let's
consider, for a moment, the prehistory of media proper—
premedia history, if you will. Let us briefly consider the standard
Western theater. Modern theatrical proscenial arches, like the
huge, screenal *scaenae frons* of ancient Roman theaters (and the
triumphal arches they arguably cite), are in some sense historical
back-media—old media, if you will. That is, proscenial arches are
arguably a branch of ancient predecessor to the now ubiquitous
mediatic screen. In modern theater, what happens on the stage
(as if upon the screen, or within the premodern *skēnē,* to use the
Greek) is considered the modern theater's product. The playing
of a drama is what is sold by theater producers and purchased
for consumption by participant audience members, much as
access to what happens on a screen is the primary consumable
of many media objects. But what happens backstage, or *obscaena*
("offstage," to use the Latin that employs the Greek), is also
theater. Without it, there would be no theater. And so "component
labor" would be an apt if awkward phrasing for the "hands" of
stagehands. Thinking of the root of the word *manufacture* as
making with hands, stagehands are operational components of
the theater made, even if they don't appear as such in the product,
such as it is. Clearly, live theater and the laboring stagehands that
support the scene/screen are not exactly identical to the iPhone
in your hand, and yet bending if not forcing our analogy might
allow us to see the iPhone through the long, shadowy, but thriving
obsolescence of the proscenial arch, the Roman *scaenae frons,*
the Triumphal arch, and other empiric backstories to the mediatic
screen. Such a diffractive gaze across media "old" and "new"
might allow us to ask whether the offstage (or in-factory) aspect
of media's making can also be considered to remain the scene of
mediatic display. The laboring bodies *obscaena,* or offscreen, are
not just your own laboring fingers at the keyboard but others and
others and others—and perhaps all of these hands are component

parts. Are they in some sense also media remains, as hand sloughs to hand sloughs to hand? Are the laborers Parikka mentions in the mines and factories in some *obscene* sense also at hand when you take your phone in hand, circulating as affective remain in the deep time of media's making? And if we were to think about that further, what would we think?

What this line of thought suggests is that the bodies of laborers remain in media objects, present as residual affective residues attached to the material components those bodies had labored to manufacture. Might the touch of a body, the sweat of it, even the sound or gesture of it in some way remain as residue of/as the device itself, in the ongoing afterlife of contact? As Roger Caillois following James George Frazer wrote provocatively of cross-species mimicry, and as Michael Taussig reinvigorated as a concept in *Mimesis and Alterity,* "things that have once been in contact remain united" (Caillois [1935] 1984, 25; Taussig 1993, 47–57). Might the touch, the sweat, the sound or smell of a body—even a laborer or a user at some distance—remain as residue, even immaterial gestural residue, of/as the device itself? Might labor and use be remains, as act(s) that recur, even if the residue of that act or those acts is buried, like ancient Roman curse tablets, within the minor architecture of each device?[7] If we think about the intra-in-animation of media in the lives not only of miners, factory workers, retailers, and other laborers but also of consumers or operators or even passers-by who engage with media devices or are otherwise actants, willing or not, in media events, is it possible to think of those bodies, too, as components?

Clearly attention to the "sticky" residue and resonant aftereffects of manufacture extend a media object off of itself into the broader scene of its hand-lings and mark said object as participant in ritu-als, habits, and encounters called "use" that result, across bodies, in remains.[8] Bodies making, bodies using, and bodies discarding all haunt and impend upon any device. In such a scene, media devices become, as human bodies do for Judith Butler (1988, 523), composed of "sedimented acts" that constitute and reconstitute bodies in relation. After all, that which is *sedimented* is a kind of geologic remain.

Of course, if the live body and geologic matter are both prehistorical matter of media, they compose a prehistory that is decidedly *ongoing* in and as media remains. It is, in fact, the ongoingness of prehistory, like the ongoingness of obsolescence, that asks us to alter our orientations to what constitutes "new" and what "old." If prehistory is also new, and the new also obsolete, what does this make of our register of the so-called march of progress, let alone our orientation to linear time that so-called progress and its alignment with the development narratives of capital invents?

The Scandal of the Obsolete

The live human biobody is nothing new. It sloughs and regenerates across generations, moving perhaps much like the geologic matter to which it also returns as it ebbs and flows between living and nonliving materials across millennia. And yet, in media and performance scholarship, and despite the regeneracy of flesh, "the body" is most often approached as disappearing, ephemeral, and locked in a present moment of a continually instantaneous "now." We do not often consider the ephemeral to be, as Wendy Chun (2011, 170–73) astutely put it, "enduring." Endurance and ephemerality have more commonly appeared as mutually exclusive opposites. And yet, slough happens—fast or slow. The rapid slough of skin cells and the slower slough of stone might suggest that ephemerality and endurance are simply matters of temporal and material scale. Shifting scales and looking to geologic drift through the lens of ecological vulnerability, stone can be seen to be ephemeral. Shifting scale and considering flesh as regenerative, life can be seen as enduring. Even the rubric "liveness" or "vitality" extends to matter formerly considered inanimate or inert when scales are shifted between the molar and the molecular or when viewed through the "singularities and haecceities" of an animistic–agentic lens of analysis (Deleuze and Guattari 1987, 408; see also Harvey 2005; Ingold 2006; Bennett 2010).

Perhaps because the live body is not commonly seen as material of extensive duration, the body itself is not considered a means to extension (and as such, it is not read as itself *already* mediatic). Beyond the supposedly limited reach of the hand's grasp (Stiegler) or supposedly limited optics of the unaided eye (Krauss after Benjamin), the body as bio-organism is often considered limited when compared to what technology can offer. This is, of course, an Enlightenment inheritance. Such assumptions not only miss the co-constitutive intra-activity of human biology with other matter (Haraway 2003; Cooper 2008; Barad 2007) but also dismiss culturally variant bodily practices of extension by which the hand is extended well beyond the grasp, so to speak. Modes of extending the body through "spirit travel" (Kapchan 2007), possession trance (Keller 2001; Harvey 2005), and breath-work, or what Aston T. Crawley (2016, 28), writing of Blackpentacostal breath, has called "complex modes of fleshly disembodiment," have often historically been labeled primitive or scandalously "savage" and dismissed as the antithesis of reason, knowledge, and even decency. Suffice to say here that the geopolitical histories of colonial expansion that labeled some embodied performance traditions of the extended body as "savage" are well known, often deeply racialized, and not beside the point for this inquiry into remains. That said, and in relation to the limits placed on the body in the interests of Enlightenment colonialists, the primitivist gaze of the Modern West has also and simultaneously fetishized the biobody, essentializing it as authentic in distinction to technology (when not romanticizing it, and live performance, as disappearing).[9] My point here is that the biobody is not customarily considered mediatic itself, not itself a means for extension and the brokering of experience. Customarily, media extend the body, not the other way around.

Of course, custom can be flipped or shaken, and alternatives to capital-colonial habits can resurge.[10] Just as, customarily, a parasite is seen to ride a host (and not the other way around), flipping the orientation of "who rides whom," or stepping to the side of a binary opposition, can raise purposefully disorienting questions, often born of disidentification with norms (Muñoz 1999; Serres 2013; Chen 2012). Rather than habitually assume that the new replaces the old, what if we consider that it may be the outmode that repeatedly replaces or subsumes or interpellates the new?[11] Each so-called new is essentially the new outmode according to habit (Chun 2016b). In the chiasmic logic of performance-based surrogation—"The King is dead, long live the King" (Roach 1996)— both ends of the chiasm are true simultaneously. Obsolescence, in this sense, is far from vanished but both produces and consumes the new at its own (bodily) bleeding edge. At this bleeding edge, the body appears to *remain* as the master of the slough—itself *both* the proud signature of the Stelarcian becoming-obsolete *and* simultaneously refusing to vanish. This is not to reessentialize or reromanticize the human biobody, which obviously changes over time and regenerates over generations, but is simply to say that the biobody is rarely seen as a reemergent residual, a medium (if not *the* medium) of regenerative obsolescence.[12] Certainly, hand to hand, bone bit after bone bit, bodies keep on circulating the currencies (various media of passage all brokering experience) that they serve to extend. That is, bodies are the extension machines for media, and obsolescence is the mode of that extension.

Perhaps we can begin to see a question emerging in the shape of these ideas. Is the body intermediary in the slough of machine upon machine, prosthetic upon prosthetic? As such, is body a media remain? And, what if obsolescence is a bodily medium? Babette B. Tischleder and Sarah Wasserman (2015, 1–2) remind us,

> Obsolescence is fundamental to our consumer practices, our relationship to objects, and our everyday lives, and yet we reflect on it so infrequently. . . . Consumer culture most robustly developed in postwar North America fetishizes the new and consequently pushes obsolescence to the margins of our attention . . . but the scandal of the obsolete is precisely that it does not vanish.

The scandal of the obsolete is precisely that it isn't.

Bone in Hand

I first saw the bone-faced bit on my computer screen as an image, sent to me in an email from Hollis Mickey with an invitation to think about the artifact further with curators at the Rhode Island School of Design (RISD) Museum of Art in Providence, where the bone now lives. At the time, it was fourteen years into the second millennium since the birth of Jesus Christ, as these things continue with the full-on force of habit to be counted, and I made my way downhill from Brown University, where I work, to the RISD museum to see the bone "live," as it were.

The bone lives in a drawer in the basement of the museum. It is not on display, so it has to be taken out of the drawer. Curator Gina Borromeo takes a small box out of the drawer and takes off the lid. She hands the box to me, together with the plastic gloves I can use to "touch" the object inside.

I extend a hand.

I'm initially sad that I can't meet the bone precisely pore to pore. But as I reach out and pick it up, I almost *feel in advance* its certain smoothness. In the hollow of my hand, right through the screenal plastic, I feel its minor weight. It strikes me that one historical thing we can know about this object is clearly still true: the token would have sat perfectly in the palm of a hand in the first century BCE just as it does so today. Then, as now, it can easily pass, hand to hand, like a coin. Even through the palm-face of plastic, I feel this aspect of its currency. It is made to pass.

With Christianity still well in the "space off" of its future, the bone was carved when Rome had not yet scorned the theater for what St. Augustine would call its obvious paganisms. The "something's coming" of the wee actor's cry might reference any number of tragic scenes mimicked, as the mask itself mimics, Greek theatrical practices. Such practices had been appropriated to the heart of the Roman Empire over a century before. On the tragic Greek stage, horrifying events arrive onstage by the medium of a messenger,

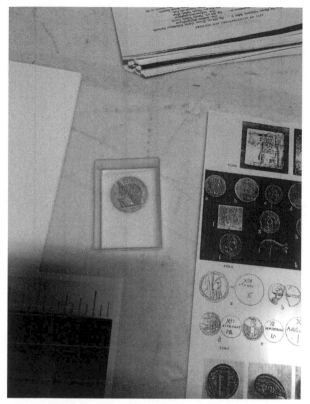

[Figure 2.2.] *Gaming Piece* in its box at the Museum of Art, Rhode Island School of Design, 2014. Photograph by the author.

boldly telling what no man has told before of what had already occurred but has yet to be encountered. In Greek tragic practice, something of the past recurs to hit with the full force of new(s) only belatedly—new only by virtue of being bygone. Restaging Greek tragedies, Romans changed this practice to reenact the horror in full view of the audience—such as Medea murdering her children. If Oedipus still gashed his eyes out offstage to be told by a messenger, the Roman playwright Seneca had the news prompt Jocasta to kill herself onstage rather than, like Sophocles, *ob skēnē,* or offstage. But arguably either way, onstage or offstage, the horror happened (again) as a kind of "something's coming" (again), and the cry of the mask as medium brokered an already belated experience anew.

But what was brokered of that experience in the basement of the RISD museum through the ongoing obsolescence machine that is both theater and new media?

Of course, that event in the basement—in which Gina hands me a bone disk in a box and I take it into my hand—was a live event. At least it was a live event in that while I was there I was living and ex- periencing an encounter with the disk contingent to the archive in the cellar in the museum in Providence in the twenty-first century. But the question is complex. If the coin (let's call it that for now) is part of an ongoing scene—let's say not only my "now" in the bowels of RISD but, say, the long Roman Empire—then the bone face and I are both playing a part in an ongoing, deep-time, *live* scene. I have entered, from the side as it were, into a scene of extended circulation. Of course, it is not really such a stretch to claim this duration. The degree to which we live in the twenty-first-century, late-capitalist "developed" world is the degree to which we are sol- idly what Derrida and Vattimo (1998, 11) called "globalatinized" (see also Mignolo 2005, 92; Agamben 2011). This is to say that detritus of the Roman Empire includes the living—many of our habits, our gestures, the words we use, many of our assumptions, circulate in the ongoing gyre of empire, bits of empire's gestic jetsam, much as this bit of bone has been doing. This is one way of suggesting that we still live within the empiric purview of this small masked player, just as we still live in the shadow of triumphal arches. If we live in that empire, not only among its ruins but *as* its ruins, living ruins, then who is to parse one liveness from another, one inanimacy from another? We cannot completely separate, in this sense, the being "live" in the time of the ongoing scene of the bone from the being alive of Gina and I there in that small room with it.

[Figure 2.3.] Curator Gina Borromeo working at the Museum of Art, Rhode Island School of Design, 2014. Photograph by the author.

Gina, I, the bone, the plastic gloves, the light, the table, the room itself are all a part of this liveness or livingness, this enduring ephemeral, this coming round again, in a basement scene offstage from the museum proper. And as momentary as it was (our meeting with the bone lasted an hour) and banal (as an archivist, Gina does this kind of work every day), it was also a scene of significant duration, spanning millennia, in which this bit of bone has been extended hand to hand to hand and in which hands have reached out to receive it.

What residue of hand, sedimentation of use, drags along with this object? And what sedimentation of use remains in hand? If now it is a "relic" lodged in the little box before us, of what other scenes and other uses, now long obsolete, does the little tongue tell?

Scholars have variously called similar bone disks coins, game tokens, or theater tickets. Today, as mentioned, the disk has value as a museum artifact. It is not exchanged anymore as a coin or a ticket for goods or services or as a surrogate for the player of a board game. It is passed, today, as art. In this scene, the bone stands as evidence of other scenes nested in sets of historical contingencies that are scripted to be long past. If it had been a coin, the exchange rate has changed. If a theater ticket, the show has long closed. If a game token, then the rules have changed. And yet, these stories attach, like bits upon bits, with the assumption that the disk began its journey at the hands of a human and will end it in safe keeping in the house of preservation that is the RISD museum, protected in plastic from the sloughing hands, hands after hands, of archivists, inquirers, and time-traveling explorers.

But wait. There may be more to the basement scene. The small face of the actor looks through the small face of the mask at something stage right. Where bone, as discrete object, begins and ends there in the basement may be undone by the gesture, made explicit at the face of it, to the space off. Something's going. Or something's coming.

Begins and ends: think of the appearance of this bone in utero, nested within an animal fetus within an animal mother, following a scripted molecular drama of other bones in other animal bodies in other times. This bone script then becoming bone in utero, as part of a bigger bone being of animal species, repeating itself across generations. Think, too, of the bones of the human hand encountering the animal bone. Imagine the first hands to carve this little bone, to feel its little tongue and enable its possible words. Bone separated from bone by the flesh of fingers. The bones of those particular human hands have likely long turned to dust and circulate on air or, better, jumped to other hands through body-to-body training, body-to-body transmission of skills. That is, even if the particular animal body and human hands that came together to fashion this disk have passed away, the work of those hands, that is, the handicraft of carving, may have been passed on as *technē*— embodied physical training—and thus remain. *Those* hands, hands that carve, hands that hold, hands that pass—those very hands, if hands are not discrete, that made the bone may yet remain. And which, one might ask, is older? More resilient? Less ephemeral? More at risk? Bone disk, or flesh hand? Or is the question of origins absurd, when attention, as the bone instructs, might better turn to the side—to the passerby, passing—bone to bone to bone, hand to hand to hand? Trajectories of liveness that exist in and as our intervals, cross matter, of encounter.

Gina and I pass the small disc back and forth between us as we discuss it together. Was it a ticket? A coin? "We don't really know what it actually was," says my host, "but," she says, "it was not a coin." She is adamant about this, though I beg to differ. I'd read someone who claimed coinage, I told her. It may have been a "theater ticket," as theater historian and classical scholar Margarete Bieber (1961, 247) would name such objects. Others, like Elizabeth Alföldi-Rosenbaum (1971, 1–9), would see such *"tesserae"* as game counters used either on mobile game boards or on mosaic games sedimented in place. But if indeed it were a game counter, that fact would not necessarily cancel its use as coinage, for, as Archer St. Clair (2003, 111) argues, gaming pieces were "undoubtedly used in commerce and as gambling tokens as well." And theater? Alföldi-Rosenbaum, adamant that the tokens are not coins, also adamantly argues against Bieber, claiming the tokens have "no relationship to the theater" (Spielman 2012, 21).

No relationship to theater?

The tiny actor's masked face would wink at me if it could, I think. In any way, it clearly suggests otherwise. Something of ancient new media of Greek theater persists in the object even if the object was not used in the theaters themselves or exchanged exactly like tickets or coins. For, of course, something of gaming, and of circulation and exchange, belongs as much to theater as it does to coinage. Jennifer Wise (2000, 181) argues in *Dionysus Writes,* "The rise in the use of coinage just prior to the appearance of drama helped determine that the theatrical stage was, and remains, a mercantile space." A space for exchange. In fact, upstairs in the RISD collection, a coin from Naxos winks at me from behind a glass case. Dionysus, the god of theater, is on one side, Silenus, his chief satyr, on the other. In this case, coinage and theater are (literally) flip sides of the same coin. At the very least, the small bone token, as artifact, invites us to recalibrate our contemporary understanding of theater and art to a more ancient worldview when theater and game were not distinct—there could be no medial specificity between theater and game—as we sometimes imagine a specificity of media or frame distinguishing high art and popular sport today. The great theater festivals in Greece were, after all, competitions. In the vibrant world of variety entertainment in Rome, competition for favor from audiences could reach fevered peaks. And as Renaissance historian Stephen Greenblatt (1989, 1–20) has claimed, wherever art events flourish one can find the "circulation of social energy" that also motivates economic exchange—the passing of coins from hand to hand.

But Gina and I were not at the City Dionysia exactly. We were in the basement of the museum. And the player we were considering— his tongue still flickering—was not "live" in the conventional sense. We couldn't quite see what the bone face sees, couldn't quite hear what it hears. Held in the palm of a human hand, the little masked bone face might "see" a wide arc of fingers, or, turned toward the palm, the little mask might "see" the rutted crease of a fleshy lifeline—if, that is, objects participate as sensate participants in events, vulnerable to the touch and touching our vulnerabilities. And why not? As Slavoj Žižek (1992, 125, emphasis added) intones, wearing a mask of Jacques Lacan, "I can never see the [object] at the point from which *it is gazing at me.*" And in this case, the object looks at me through a mask that looks away.

Something's coming! it cries, hailing the tragedies it reiterates through its gesture to the space off.

At the margins of our attention, in the *obscaena*, the "something's coming" may simply be the past: what Michel de Certeau (1984, 5) might term the "oceanic rumble" of the accumulative everyday, or hail of the trash heap pile-up of the so-called obsolescent that

arrests Benjamin's Angel of Progress in backward flight. Thus,
rather than new media sloughing the body or rendering it obsolete,
we might also and *simultaneously* consider the relation the other
way around, backward, or to the side of the dream of progress that
still haunts our orientation to "the new." If media and the body at
hand are intrainanimate, or deeply entangled as hand-as-tool/tool-
as-hand, how can one be said to predate or out-remain the other?
This question concerns the persistence of the outmode over time,
that is, the fact that obsolescence just keeps on keeping on, moving
in multiple directions in the (deep) time of an extended now and
jumping media as fast and faster than outmoded media materials
can gather in the rumbling Pacific Gyre.

Some readers may already be calling out from their reading, Oh,
no! Something's going! While it is true that some of us have been
working to expand the frame of photography, for example, from
the sole purview of the nineteenth-century discovery of "chemicals
of capture" to find it in the ancient and prehistoric, such as in the
regenerative and citational still of "the pose," few scholarly works
are devoted to the backward or sideways step of technology—
ancient Greek film, Neolithic video, or Paleolithic digital arts! One
of the implications of thinking media in deep time and relative to
"remains" concerns the unsettling of prior categories delimiting
"liveness" and "duration." Where previously we had considered live
events to conclude when an actor leaves the stage (for instance),
and despite some performance artists like Linda Montano or
Tehching Hsieh making live art durational pieces over many years
(Gonzalez Rice 2016; Heathfield 2015), we have not often asked
whether a piece of live art can be considered to extend for, say,
forty thousand years and more. Can a medial event (an event
brokered through an intermediary) travel backward and forward in
time, traversing billions of years ongoing? The logic of liveness as
ephemeral that dominated performance studies in the twentieth
and early twenty-first centuries assumed that live arts, such as
theater, dance, and performance-based arts, have nothing to give
to the archive except by-products, such as photographs, playbills,

videos, or ticket stubs, which are not (so the old argument went) the *performance* itself. Bodily performance itself disappeared and only the material detritus of its outmode remained. The body was not a mode of remaining but a mechanism not only of obsolescence but of disappearance. And yet, as cited earlier, "the scandal of the obsolete is precisely that it does not vanish."

As I argued in *Performing Remains: Art and War in Times of Theatrical Reenactment,* bodily practices, sedimented sets of physical habits, in-body techniques, and various modes of physical training remain such that performance-based arts recur. Gesture is, as Marcel Maus made clear, a bodily technique of (re)iteration, capable of jumping bodies, jumping matter, and riding the current of "new" emergence even as gesture, dragged always from the past as iterative, is never new but always essentially reemergent (Noland 2009, 16). Rather, gesture's essential iterativity (which is to say its capacity to be reiterated) simultaneously cites *and* opens out toward "something's coming." This is another way of saying that gesture is emergent and obsolescent simultaneously. As such, the detritus of performance and media event is as much the live body (capable of gesturing again, as gestures jump body to body) as it is the recorded documentation or artifactual evidence or brokering technologies of that event. This is to say that the hand is a *remain* of the live event of a handshake, even as it is also the script and medium for a new or another hand held in the future. Similarly, relative to the remains of a handheld device like an iPhone, tossed aside when traded up for a newer model, it is possible to argue that the hand that tosses the device aside nevertheless remains as component part.

The hand, then, is a component part of both newness and obsolescence. Even as the hand sloughs skin year after year, and hands regenerate generation after generation as flesh and bone of my flesh and bone, iterations of media slough and regenerate model after model. This is not to say that "the body" is any more stable, essential, or always the same than the materials it engages or that engage it. Rather, it is to ask after the "liveness" of matter in

intrainanimate and cross-temporal mediated encounters in which
becoming and obsolescence move in multiple temporal directions
at once. The body is a mediatic remain inasmuch as obsolescence
is a bodily medium.

Inspired by Parikka's blunt statement that "media starts much
before media becomes media," one through-line of thought in this
essay is something of an excavation (if that can be the right word)
of flesh and bone as remainders of mediatic beginnings, but
also as continual surrogates (or remains that recur and replace,
replace and recur). What kind of (obsolete emergent) remainder
is the human in the entanglement of human and nonhuman that
is (rapidly sloughing) media? Or, why is the so-called human so
persistently slow in its obsolescence and media so quick to slough?
That is, despite continual proclamations of the posthuman and
deepening new materialist attempts to explore our constitutive
entanglements with the nonhuman, why is the humanist orientation so slow to slough?

We know that the rapid becoming obsolescence of technology,
enabled as humans pass our media hand to hand to hand to trash,
contributes to the piles of electronic waste that, as one report put
it, could "fill a line of 40-ton trucks that, end-to-end, would stretch
three-quarters of the way around the world," or in the words of
Achim Steiner when he served as executive director of the UN
Environment Programme, a "tsunami of e-waste rolling out over
the world" (UNNC 2015). Even as the ecological problems we face
in relationship to human waste are problems we must take in hand
in that they demand handling, we have trouble accounting for the
ongoing *bodily remains* of media—which is one way of saying that
outmoded media are still *in our hands,* even when tossed aside as
obsolete. Again, this is not to offer the human as primary or essential or even as predating the tool. This is also not to present the
hand, as Heidegger did, as some exemplary emblem of humanism,
thus holding tight to an (obsolete?) animacy hierarchy in which
humans are privileged evolutionary agents of progress. Quite the
contrary. The animacy hierarchy with human at the apex will soon,

one hopes, crash and burn as a remnant of the delusions of the deadly Anthropocene. Contemporary new materialisms point us toward nonhuman and human entanglements in molecular and molar worldmakings. Such decolonial neoanimisms seek to actively remove (historically white) humans off of any apex and into intra-active, intra-agential relational conglomerates with matter and media. Human circulates with, as, and among other animate and inanimate beings, including the multiple media that "we" extend and subtend, and that extend and subtend "us" in ongoing dramas of mutual surrogation. "We" are (still) hand in hand with "our" media and with "our" planet. Even outmoded media are still in our hands, just as billion-year-old bits of rock compose our handhelds. And "we" humans also remain in their hands—the hands of rock, the hands of mineral, the hands of water, the hands of air, the hands of handhelds.[13]

In fact, the outmode is precisely what remains. What I aim to suggest here is that one thing potentially excavated by media archaeology would be a remainder component integral to the device, still afloat in the ocean of obsolescence that is the late modern world: the live bio-user, the body as remain. Just as no-longer-live bio-users compose the matter of oceans, earth, and air, and mingle with the remains of objects, so too the matter of oceans, earth, and air compose the hands that hold the tool, the tools that hold the hand. It is the ongoingness of such remains, as matter transmogrifies to matter, that informs the circulating deep and oceanic time of *human* history as well as the deep-time history of all matter as such. I am reminded of Christina Sharpe's (2016) *In the Wake: On Blackness and Being,* particularly her lyrical writing about ongoing remains in the violent historical afterflow of the Middle Passage. The Middle Passage, of course, refers to the shipping routes of the flesh trade that afforded the exploitive extraction and circum-Atlantic circulation of humans (and nonhumans animals and things) from Africa to the "New" world for the purposes of slave labor to benefit the empiric projects of white settler colonials. Writing of what happened to the bodies of Africans that were

tossed or jumped overboard en route, Sharpe writes of the disinte-
gration and reintegration of their biological matter, citing ancestral
remains *as ongoingness* in the material flows of the world that we
sense, feel, and otherwise know. The atoms of those people, she
writes, "are out there in the ocean even today." In the wake of the
past, Sharpe intones, the past is not past but "still with us" (40,
62). And thus we recall, again, that the scandal of the obsolete is
precisely that it is not.

Intrainanimacy

In general, I am interested in the reverberant life of so-called
obsolete or vestigial media, including theater, film, TV, Paleolithic
rock art, body art, live art, and all other media on the flip side of
the new. These are media not at the bleeding edge of the new but
deeply embedded or wrapped in the congealed skin curtain of
the outmode. Theater is particularly interesting, as it is, arguably,
one of the most obsolete media imaginable, and yet, live, you just
can't kill it (and some would argue that this is because it is already
dead; Schneider 2011). Policing the boundaries between "live" art
and recorded or otherwise nonlive work is, however, extremely
difficult, especially when live performance is itself often composed
of the dead, or, better said, a medium for letting the dead play
back across the bodies of the living. Examples are legion, but think
simply of Hamlet's father's ghost, not to mention hosts of (so-called
"primitive" or obsolescent) practices of possession trance by which
ancestors revisit to ride the bodies of the living for a time. In *Hamlet,* the dead king returns to set the record straight, rendering the
live and the record in inverse relationship to the simplistic claim
that theater is live in distinction to a recording, or other mechanics
of the trace. The trace, like the dead, can take place live, and the
live can take place dead (so to speak), befuddling distinctions
between animacy and inanimacy that have differentiated medial
technologies from live bodies in the past.

Across my recent work, I have been arguing that liveness is as
much a ruse as deadness, inanimacy as much a ruse as animacy.

We might also say that "old" is as much a ruse as "new," new as old. When the border between live acts and mediated acts comes undone, so too do other borders follow—such as our habituation to distinguishing old from new. We are only as live, or as nonlive, as our habits of parsing such distinctions instruct. Such distinctions simultaneously delimit an "us" from a "them" or an "I" from an "it." As Mel Y. Chen unpacks in their careful historicizing of humanist animacy hierarchies in *Animacies,* transgressing those limits or upsetting those hierarchies with something like "inanimate life" queers both terms—*both* animate *and* inanimate (Chen 2012, 11, 23–55). Chen suggests that rather than work to reinvest certain materialities with life, as a great deal of vitalist new materialism proposes (such as Bennett 2009), we might instead "remap live and dead zones away from those very terms, leveraging ani-macy toward a consideration of affect in its queered and raced formations" (11).

As suggested in the previous section, I have recently been working to remap interinanimacy toward *intra*(in)animacy, following new materialists like Karen Barad following Donna Haraway. Intrainan-imacy might better touch the slip and slide of our amongnesses, besidenesses, withnesses, and againnesses and resist delimiting us, as the prefix *inter-* might be said to do, to an essentialized "betweenness." Does the prefix *inter-* problematically tend to replay a particular Western agonic relation between traditionally binarized terms, otherwise known as the progress-oriented tool of the dialec-tic by which dyads like savage–civilized or old–new are continually pitted in a master–slave battle for hierarchical "recognition"?[14] Might *intra-* as prefix better disorient habitual relations among binarized terms, such as *live* and *dead* or *animate* and *inanimate,* and resist pitting two poles against each other in bicameral, agonic battle?

As I said at the start of this section, there is little on this earth more outmoded than the live theater. I've decided to engage by quoting myself—a particularly theatrical thing to do, like an academic selfie or a mask of a face atop a face:

Live theatre has long imagined itself to be dead. Cinema was said to have killed it again, after a precedent slaying by photography. In the long march of "new technology" theatre is the card-carrying bearer of obsolescence. It even kills itself. Its modern visionaries of note—Zola, Stanislavsky, Artaud—constantly descried the habit of theatre's *own* conventions to strangle it from within. Theatre, it appears, has long been its own voracious parasite and the source of its own perpetual ruin. It's dead, but, already dead, you just can't kill it. Any artwork that traffics in theatre or the theatrical (which is not the same as performance or the performative) can be ruined by that traffic, or (worse by some accounts) can be traffic in ruin. We can track a persistent investment in theatre's ruin value running through visual art and media history as well. It's the decay we love to hate. The decay that just won't quit. The theatrical—tinged always with the feminine, the queer, the undead, and the live body—is always there when you look again. (Schneider 2012, 159)

To see what updates I may or may not have made in the citation, you would need to engage the "original" through whatever technology you use to display my prior iteration to yourself. Hand to hand, device to device, citation is a kind of orature of access passed through sloughing technologies, air-brushed and exfoliated again and again, transmitted through generations of media as if through the mouthpieces of masks or across the flickering tongues of generations of actors replacing each other like models of iPhones. "Speak the speech, I pray you, as I pronounced it to you," says Hamlet to his actors as they prepare to launch a play through the device of their theatrical craft, "trippingly on the tongue." The trip of this speech, like the flick of the tongue or the gesture of a hand in motion, passes through actor, folio, book, movie projector, digital screen, and back to hand, again and again. What remains is a gesture that jumps. What is handed over and across, through and as media, becomes obsolescence at and as the pass.

The study of theater is the study, one could suggest, of the regeneration of outmodedness. To re-play Seneca's *Oedipus,* for example, might be to deploy the latest immersive technologies to have an audience of users feel most alive as Jocasta becomes most dead onstage (or vice versa). This is not only because our "newest" technologies often support the past in play but because rooting around in screenal culture's ongoing prehistories, we find, I submit, that the past is alive and well in the ongoing guise of obsolescence. The triumphal arch of the Roman Empire, for instance, is not so much *over and gone* or even *vanished* as it is *remaining* to recirculate as computer screen. Having extended the optical geometries of perspective from Vesuvius to Alberti to the camera to the digital image, might the empiric technology of the threshold that the triumphal arch pronounces in some sense remain, an ongoing gesture perhaps, resonating at the pass in the computer's screen? If the arch has *passed on to remain* and recirculate as a device for screening, does the digital screen drag something of empire and empiric relations along with it? And is that empiric "something" that the screen contains make something of an elemental gesture, relative to bodies that organize themselves in quotidian relationship to screens? Could the following question be at all appropriate: Is the triumphal arch a component remainder, a bit of material in an ongoing scene, resident in the screen as such, much as my prior citation is resident in this text? But let's not stop in Rome. We can, of course, make the "new" even older. If Kaja Silverman (1995, 195) sees the liminal, threshold form of film prefigured on the Paleolithic cave wall, as she does in *Threshold of the Visible World,* are we limited to thinking of the Paleolithic as vanished, or might we think instead of that obsolescence (like prehistory itself) as *ongoing*? And if so, would this make Paleolithic art a media remain? And possibly even make it *live*?

You will recall that one of the questions that arose in the RISD museum basement, with the bit of bone in my hand, was whether that bone was live and what might be accomplished by even posing that question. The pursuit of this question in part concerns the

historical boundaries problematically separating so-called live art
(such as theater or dance) from art formerly known as object based
or media based, with materiality and media or technology sometimes standing in unsupportable distinction to liveness or to the
bio-actor. There have been many debates on this that need not be
rehearsed here, for surely the old borders separating the supposed
liveness of the human actor from the recordedness, traceness,
prostheticness (pick your antonym for *live*) of technological media
or apparatuses of capture have not been fully operational for some
time.[15] But still, what to make of the proposition that the bone disk
is live? That it is a "scriptive thing," in Robin Bernstein's (2009, 69)
sense, is easy to accept. As such, the disk exists as an event in its
passage hand to hand to hand and is implicated, intimately, with
the live bodies that it engages and that engage it. We can perhaps
allow that, in hand, it intra(in)animates—hand becoming tool, tool
becoming hand—or consists in the overlay of hand with tool (both
hand and tool being hand, both hand and tool being tool). Allowing
as much might give the bit of bone an agency that moves off of
individual materiality and into that materiality's intra-actions, its
withnesses, its trajectories, that thus extend its being to the gyre in
which it circulates. It circulates as material with other material, as
debris with other debris. It circulates for a moment with my hand,
if my hand (holding bone) is as much debris as this little two-faced
shard. Thinking this way, we give to the bone the flesh that passes
it, while giving to the flesh the bone that it passes. Which comes
first or which lasts longer, bone token or flesh gesture, becomes
a less interesting question than questions that would seek to
account for intrainanimation. The bit of debris takes place as its
circulation—whether human to human, human to object, object to
human, or object to object. Like deciding for priority, deciding for
animacy or inanimacy begins to feel moot.

In her 2003 essay "Posthumanist Performativity: Toward an Understanding of How Matter Comes to Matter," Barad distinguished
interaction from intra-action:

The notion of *intra-action* (in contrast to the usual "inter-action," which presumes the prior existence of independent entities/relata) represents a profound conceptual shift. It is through specific agential intra-actions that the boundaries and properties of the "components" of phenomena become determinate and that particular embodied concepts become meaningful. A specific intra-action (involving a specific material configuration of the "apparatus of observation") enacts an *agential cut* (in contrast to the Cartesian cut—an inherent distinction—between subject and object) effecting [rather than rendering inherent] a separation between "subject" and "object." (815)

Adopting intra- for intrainanimation, we might say that animate and inanimate *both* differentiate *and* cobecome each other through a cut, or interval, in and as relation without the resultant distinction among intra-actants being essentially prior to or inherent in the interval of their exchange. For example, writing of living with mercury in an experience of "mercury poisoning," Chen relates to sharing animacy and inanimacy with the mineral they host. Deciding which was living their life—Chen or the mineral—becomes impossible to parse in what they term a queer intimacy. Each becomes each other. Each looks out through the other's eyes—not so much interacting as intra-acting. That our intra-actions may be mimetic (which is not to say representational) as we cross-become each other across difference, and as and through our media, is key to thinking of intra-actions as *reiterative.* Again Barad: "matter does not refer to a fixed substance; rather, *matter is substance in its intra-active becoming—not a thing, but a doing, a congealing of agency. Matter is a stabilizing and destabilizing process of iterative intra-activity*" (822, emphasis original). You may note that I used the word "reiterative" in advance of Barad's "iterative." I did this because, in fact, the dictionary definition of *iterate* is, precisely, "to perform or utter repeatedly." Iteration is always already reiteration, and reiteration is iteration. Repetition is a mode of becoming that pronounces a cut and, paradoxically perhaps, always (re)opens a door for difference.

In *Agency and Embodiment,* Carrie Noland (2009) not only gives us
live embodied gestures—handwork so to speak—as technologies
of iterability but offers a corrective, through paleoethnographer
André Leroi-Gourhan, to some habits of thinking about technological media in distinction to bio-users. Noland reminds us
that media theorists, writing about writing and media, relied on
Leroi-Gourhan's paleoethnography as they crafted their argument
that one cannot envision human nature outside of its constitutive
relation to *technology* or prosthetic tools. Using Leroi-Gourhan,
they posited that "humans come to have the bodies they have, are
embodied in a specific way, through formative interaction with . . .
prosthetic tools." But, Noland argues, when emphasis is placed on
the prosthetic of tools, some media theory tends to neglect Leroi-
Gourhan's "equally forceful emphasis on the gesture manipulating
those tools," the tools *in hand,* as it were, and thus privilege one
side of the equation in a straight linear development. They occlude,
she argues, intra-activity—the paleontologist's emphasis "on the
lived, somatic-kinesthetic experience." Not only is the gesturing,
tool-using hand already, for Leroi-Gourhan, itself a tool (a tool the
ethnographer gives to animality in general) but the tool used by
the hand is, foremost, a gesture—*gestures*—and the gesture makes
the hand as much as the hand makes the gesture (Noland 2009,
94).[16] And gesture, Avita Ronell tells us, always inaugurates relation,
or, we could stay, instantiates an interval for passage, however
infinitesimal (microsecond) or broad (forty thousand years).

Hand in Rock in Hand

The hand that touches is also the hand that is touched—to recall
Husserl's famous image—and thinking about the chiasm that this
emblematizes, the result for Merleau-Ponty will be that the future
is past and the past future. In any case, and again following the
logic of the chiasm, can we think of the cave wall as, perhaps,
calling to the hand to use it, as much as the hand extending toward
the rock face? Or can we think of the painter's hand as the cave's
prosthetic extension, its tool, perhaps? If we ignore the human

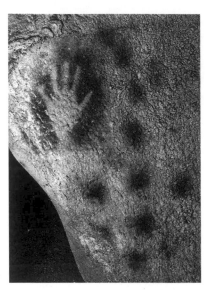

Figure 2.4. Pech Merle Hand, Paleolithic, Lot, France. Photograph from Wikimedia Commons.

entirely, might we listen to the stone and the red ochre of a negative hand stencil as engaged in call and response? My response, as a twenty-first-century hand at the Paleolithic scene, is to the ongoing event at an incredible speed of connectivity: forty thousand years.

Tools and bodies, like poses and bodies, gestures and objects, objects and objects, bodies and bodies co-constitute each other in and through mutual and recurrent encounters, practices, that are always iterations, constituted and reconstituted in mimetic exchange, *live. (Note: mimesis is not the same as representation.)* Liveness does not only exist on the side of the seemingly animate user of the seemingly inanimate tool but flows all the way around or, as Noland says, "both ways." Neither comes first. Or second. To separate hand and tool, or animate and inanimate, begins to appear absurd when each constitutes the other, or improvises the other, as Fred Moten (2003a) writes, or, as Chen might write, co-inhabits the other with an intimacy they call out as queer. Inter(in)animate—a word I pick out of the gyre of Moten but also adopt from John Donne—continues to resonate for me in this regard, even as I improvise changing inter to intra. In Donne's 1612 poem "The Ecstacy," the word *interinanimate* describes lovers, locked in coital embrace, so still they appear as sepulcher statues, and indeed, it is unclear in the poem whether they are actually just that. The liveness of maybe stone or the stillness of maybe live is moot at the point of ecstasy, or in the interval between their hands in which they hold each other's body. And anyway ecstasy, like the Roman mask's two-faced tragedy, perhaps always comes from the side (from the Greek *ek-stasis,* "to be or stand beside oneself").

Consider Valie Export's *Körperkonfigurationen* performances-become-photographs in which stone–flesh intimacies suggest a vulnerable living with, a mutual becoming, or a "something" not quite discernable. In these 1976 pieces, the human form is molded by the architecture, which is molded by the human form—much like the disk in hand, the hand on bone.

In this series, Valie Export placed her body in relationship to archi-techtures. The vulnerability and precarity of the body is brought into relief in relationship to the stone, but the sturdy architecture of the body is also exhibited. The relation of mutual support, and mutual vulnerability, is expressed in this work. The question of the limits of the live and the liveness of architecture appears open to engage outside of our usual habit of distinguishing animate and inanimate. In these images as I read them, intrainanimation and intravulnerability seem to arise as much from the stone as from flesh. Which makes which—which made which—is less clear than it might be. Stone is as articulate as body and body as articulate as stone—the agency in that speaking is mutual, intrainanimate, and intraactive. And note, of course: it is not as stone, bone, and flesh that these gestures make their transit to our present conversation but as photographic images very likely recomposed as digital as you hold this essay in your hand or on your screen. Stone/flesh enters your eyes through other means and, like mercury in your blood, makes physical contact with you. Again, as Caillois wrote of cross-species mimicry and as many suggest of possession trance,

Figure 2.5. Valie Export, *Theseustempel (Stufen),* 1982. Copyright Valie Export, Bildrecht Wien, 2018. Courtesy Valie Export.

Figure 2.6. Valie Export, *WVZ 229,* 1982. Copyright Valie Export, Bildrecht Wien, 2018. Courtesy Valie Export.

"things that have once been in contact remain united" (Caillois [1935] 1984, 25). And as Deleuze (1994, 199–200) wrote suggestively, though he wasn't writing of architecture, possession trance, mercury poisoning, or mimesis but of Ideas: "Another *always* thinks in me."

A standard approach to media might more eagerly chart the forward marching changes in medial technologies and media objects that mark some media as outmoded and introduce other media as emergent than look to obsolescence and newness as itself a product and defining characteristic—a remain—of media across time. The gesture to the space off necessary to mark the crisis—Something's coming! or Something's going!—is, itself, far from new, as Chun (2016b) usefully explored in *Updating to Remain the Same: Habitual New Media*. If the objects of old media are abandoned to trash heaps or given to museums, what becomes of the bodily habits those once-new objects congealed in the bodies of users? Where have they gone? Have they long been sloughed off and disappeared, or is there a mode of remaining in, say, the role of the hand in, say, a handheld object or an object passed hand to hand? Or the fact of the eye as a component part of the use of something, let's say a stereoscope—does the live eye *remain in and as* sloughed media? Is the looking itself part of looking into a stereoscope, or is holding itself part of holding the apparatus, or is the materialized action of hand-to-hand a component part of passing the stereoscope to another viewer? That is, are these material acts that enabled or surrounded the apparatus something that remain of the material technology even as the particular stereoscope is hailed as outmoded and no longer passed as frequently as, say, a TV remote or a bucket of popcorn? If so, then the irruptive performance genealogies that play across bodies in relation and still flicker in and out of use, like the tongue of the masked Roman actor, are an under-mined aspect of media archaeology.

Bone to bone and flesh to flesh sloughing and regenerating across generations, the question here concerns the role of the body in the production and dissemination of media's continually brokered cries

[Figure 2.7.] *Gaming Piece* on phone screen, 2018. Photograph by the author.

of oldness and newness. Something's coming! Something's going! Again! And again, the event will mask itself as something never before seen or experienced, something just out of reach brought close to hand, or something close to hand pressed just out of reach. Can we mark a collective thrall to the continual reproduction of obsolescence as an embodied habit of empire? Is obsolescence a physical habit, a learned experience? Is it itself is a kind of *ongoing* and *live* habit of sloughing media like skin, a gestic mode of use and refuse that could be considered a part of media's remains?

We might think of it this way: even as an object, an intermediary, such as a photograph or a coin, may be passed hand to hand, and even as that photo or coin may be exchanged for other objects, or replaced by other objects which are passed hand to hand (from coins to paper to plastic credit cards, or tintypes to snapshots to handheld digital devices), does the pass itself have any status in the scene of media, ongoing as it arguably is? Is hand that passes the handheld a remain of media, a component part, and an element in the slough of obsolescence? And even if human bodies are not the only bodies at the scene of transmission, is transmission itself—the interval of relation perhaps—*something of a medial remain*?

I am returned to the inverse of the bloody edge of obsolescence—the congealed and ever-ending repetition of the would-be bone-chilling cry, "Hey, you there, *something's coming*!" The ancient flickering tongue brokers a call that provokes me to look and look again. Run and rerun, which came first? I beam the bit of bone to you, here, as Figure 2.7.

Something's Coming—The Geologic Past

In "The Savage Curtain," episode 22 of Star Trek's third season, we find the following conversation:

SCOTT: Does that appear human to you Mr. Spock?

SPOCK: Fascinating. For a moment it appeared almost mineral, like living rock with heavy fore claws. It's settling down now to completely human readings.

SCOTT: We can beam—it—aboard at any time sir.

KIRK: Take tricorder readings and see if—it—is human. . . .

MCCOY: Human, Jim.

KIRK: Mr. President!

"Savage Curtain" first beamed into American living rooms on March 7, 1969. In that episode, set far into the future in star date 5906.4, a bit of rock from a planet deep in space "becomes" Abraham Lincoln and is encountered by the *Enterprise* crew as, indeed, their Earthling forebear. Beyond the comprehension of the crew, Lincoln materializes as *both* nonhuman rock *and* human life.

[Figure 2.8.] Lincoln encountered by the *Enterprise* crew in "The Savage Curtain," *Star Trek,* season 3, episode 22, first aired March 7, 1969.

As the rock-become-Lincoln steps aboard the *Enterprise,* is scanned and read as living, the crew switch from the pronoun "it" to "he," and the drama begins to unfold. Only the medical doctor McCoy seems suspicious. As Lincoln and Kirk head from the transporter room to the bridge, McCoy steps to the side to speak to Scotty:

> MCCOY: Just what was it you locked onto down there?
>
> SCOTT: You heard Mr. Spock yourself. Mineral he called it. Like living rock.
>
> MCCOY: And that became Lincoln.[17]
>
> SCOTT: I couldn't tell. There may have been another figure down there standing by.

This is the most we ever find out about what exactly transpires among rocks and humans on the planet. McCoy's word "became" must suffice, toggled together with Scotty's strange notion of besideness—or "standing by." At the close of the episode, as rock

[Figure 2.9.] Rock creature in "The Savage Curtain," *Star Trek,* season 3, episode 22.

appears to return to rock, we know no more about it or him or them than the capacity to stand by, and in standing by, become.

These brief bits of dialogue hail us in the twenty-first century as if from another galaxy when mid-twentieth-century, decidedly liberal neofrontierists imagined they could both "boldly go where no man has gone before" and, in so going, cause no harm.[18] They did not, however, "leave no trace." The series, which originally aired from September 1966 through June 1969 on NBC and comprises seventy-nine individual episodes, is now available for anytime viewing on a variety of internet platforms (not to mention its many offspring in series spinoffs and feature films). *Star Trek* essentially orbits our quotidian neoliberal lives like floating downloadable detritus of American exceptionalism (Feffer 2015), still proffering siren songs of a future free of the stains of violence and injustice—even while making those very historical violences repeatedly re-irrupt across our screens. Indeed, again and again we watch cast as crew boldly going where no man has gone before, only to find them repeatedly forced to acknowledge that what they "encounter" as alien is in fact their own past, which heaves itself to greet them in traumatic fits and starts, and, as in this episode, as geological drift.[19]

The historical tracks of white conquest and (settler) colonialism spread the Christo-capitalist worldview globally, planting distinctions between what constitutes live and what constitutes nonlive, what constitutes hand and what tool, who constitutes human and who nonhuman, and what constitutes old and new. Modernity fetished "new" technology and invented primitivity and obsolescence to be scattered across the globe like flags across capitalism's creeping, developing, industrializing Anthropocene.[20] Such dyadic distinctions are deeply racialized and continually march to the beat of "extractive" exploitation for capital. In *Star Trek,* the supposed opposite of empiric exploitation is peaceful exploration, and yet episode after episode tracks the often exploitive interruptions, foibles, and sheer inanity of the crew's apparent well-meaning mission. They continually encounter, in outer space, nothing but the fallacy of their own earthbound assumptions (and this is arguably the great pleasure and promise of the series for its many fans). In the midst of their incomprehension and their own admitted lack of any *logical* explanations they nevertheless rely on the half-human Spock to supply, they dig up paradox as deep-space theater in order to act out, again, the irruptive nature of their ignorance and, contra Spock, indulge their fully human emotions (affect being, here, that which appears to mark humans as humans above all).

The living rock episode, titled "Savage Curtain," finds Kirk and Spock together with rocky Lincoln, beaming back down to the planet to be greeted by a glowing molten rock creature with multiple lightbulby eyes and absurd white-gloved crab claws that they (let's use a gender-neutral pronoun) click together as they make historical personages appear. As the rock draws other historical figures onto the scene, they set them all to fighting for their "lives" (yes, they throw stones and makeshift spears at each other) in what the rock calls, explicitly, a "drama." What do you mean "drama," asks Kirk directly, clearly confused, as his life appears to be at stake. "You're an intelligent life-form," says the rock. "I'm surprised you do not see the honor we do you. Don't you perceive . . . we have created a stage identical to your own world?" Don't you perceive, your drama is your planet and your planet is alive?

I start with this rather daft example of a theater-making, crab-clawed inanimate life-form from outer space to highlight how absurd the idea of something/someone being equally inanimate and animate at once appears to the exemplary space-going liberal humanist trekkers. It's strange enough to be presented as precisely that: *alien*. And yet, at the same time, that alien *becomes* "us," *both* theatrically *and* in actuality. A debate about whether the rock-conjured historical personages were "mere" images runs across the episode but ends with Kirk's resolute and decidedly swooning declaration that, no, he feels that he "actually met Lincoln." The gleam in Kirk's eye, captured now in a close up, is meant to seduce us all to accept his juicy sphere of cross-temporal, cross-alien

Figure 2.10. Living Rock in "The Savage Curtain," *Star Trek,* season 3, episode 22.

intimacy—a signature *Star Trek* swooning that David Greven, drawing on Jack Halberstam, has recently argued makes original *Trek* come to seem "less like a sexist series and more like a text that actively solicits the queer eye" (Greven 2009, 17; Nyong'o 2015). Perhaps it is both/and. In any case, it is curious that rock become human, and human become rock, is tantamount, in this episode, to future becoming past and past future, old becoming new and new old. And indeed, the episode depends on it being unclear as to whether the future can be distinguished from the past, live from nonlive, or whether we will always be greeted by some rocky (as in vertiginous) amalgam. The *Star Trek* mineral–human intrainanimation is at once as cross-temporal as it is intraplanetary, as if "we" could not touch an inanimate life, or "it" touch "us," without simultaneously traveling both temporally and spatially across or among vast intervals we had hitherto habitually held to be nontraversable.

In 2013, I had made a trip to witness, firsthand, negative handprints made by humans in the Paleolithic in numerous caves of the Dordogne and Lot in France. I wanted to ask about the hand as hail and think about the duration of gesture and the intervals between gesture's reiterations. Might twenty-five or forty thousand years, be traversable hand to hand? If gestures are primarily "iterable techniques" (Noland 2009, 101), then how could one iteration (my hand, raised in hail) be understood in total temporal insolation from subsequent (or previous) iterations of a hand raised in hail? Iterations, after all, *require* intervals. Iterations necessarily jump— time, space, and bodies—to become themselves as gestures in reiteration. Is there a statute of limitation on response-ability?

Heading to France in 2013, I wondered, if I meet a Paleolithic hand (a first hand) with a second hand, my own, meeting that first hand firsthand, what would become of first and second? Standing in the cave, why would I be more "live," more "vital," in responding to, or even in recognizing, the Paleolithic hand than the *first hand* was/is/or continues to be in making the hail together with stone? In the logic of call and response, wouldn't response, in reverse, also initiate the hail *as* hail? Which hand makes the hail a hail?

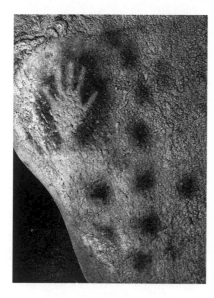

[Figure 2.11.] Pech Merle Hand, Paleolithic, Lot, France. Photograph from Wikimedia Commons.

That is, even if the cave hand wasn't "originally" a hail, does it become one—even illegitimately—by virtue of response? Or does it become, backward, a response by virtue of a hail? If I fundamentally engage the Paleolithic hand because I also have one, and respond to the gesture of the upheld palm because I also make one or might make one, does liveness, as a matter of exchange, exist only as intervallic reiteration (which is neither sameness nor difference but both)?[21] Is there then a time limit on the interval? Or on liveness?

It may be too easy to think of these teasing questions with human hands, which conveniently come to us as inversions of one and another. Can we think about the hail—an inaugurating or recycling of relation—without the human? We could excise the human from the hail entirely and ask whether the rock itself (regardless of the trace of the human) might be approached as performing a hail, moving, in deep time, with a gesture of its own cast to its own and its others. The hail is, interestingly, what W. J. T. Mitchell (2006, 37) implicitly gives to any and all images and objects in *What Do Pictures Want: The Lives and Loves of Images?* And Bernstein (2009, 69) put it extremely succinctly, writing, "Things hail." Certainly "things" hail each other with or without humans, as Caillois ([1935] 1984) astutely suggested using the word *mimesis* to discuss the intrain-animate ricochet among stick insects and twigs, twigs and insects. I like the notion of the hail because it opens and perhaps suspends or extends an interval, an opening for response, and even as it activates ideology,[22] it might also open worlds for difference (Schneider 2018).

I am concerned about thinking with the interval, opening in infinite directions both spatially and temporally, as a continual invitation for difference, because one of my concerns, reductively articulated here, is an a-historicity in the new materialist turn, a potential essentialism (an essentializing of potential), a universalizing and, if not anthropomorphizing, then a molecularizing that can rush in at the door of a generalized animacy. Rather than generalized animacy, a cross-temporal and cross-spatial interval would have to invite us *both* to reencounter history *and* to open continual emergence of the new. Call and response—situated by Thomas F. DeFrantz and Anita Gonzalez (2014, 8, 11) as a "continual unfolding of experience" and a manifestation of global "black sensibilities"— weaves past and future in intervallic resonance. To call the past to appear for account, or to be called by the past to respond with account, is to change the past as a means to change the future, just as change in the future requires a change in our habituations, our calls to and our response-abilities for our pasts. In this sense, the past is an ongoing performance of reemergent actuality, full of performance's potential and performance's drag. In the words of Maurice Merleau-Ponty (2012, 444) from the midst of his reflec-tions on in-handedness and tacility in the face of the flesh of the world, "the past, then, is not past, nor is the future future." Again, in the words of Sharpe (2016, 9), navigating the historical wake of slave ships, "in the wake, the past that is not past reappears." And obviously, for a ship named *Enterprise* (few names would sound more solidly as a moniker for capitalism), a ship that sails outer space from the midst of the Cold War to forge a wake called the future, the past that is not past reappears as the future that is not future. Past, present, and future—bygone, living, yet to come—are intra-articulate and intrapresent, composed in each other through call and response. None are animate nor inanimate, none old, none new, but a rocking, vertiginous both/and in which "matters" are both historical and emergent—open, unresolved, indeterminate, and in "our" extended hands.

For now, it is enough to keep trying to think with the extended hand at the scene of cross-temporal exchange as I stand in the cave at Pech Merle and encounter my first hand live. I want to respond. At the time, it didn't seem to me to matter what exactly was intended by the so-called human when she raised a hand to so-called rock. As some paleontologists have suggested (though others disagree), it may have been the rock that was hailing and the hand responding, or the hand that was entering or otherwise intrainanimating with rock. Cave paintings may have served as por- tals, with rock potentially *entered* through dream states of trance and by virtue of ritual—the rock, in this case, a kind of curtain or threshold to alternate galaxies of experience with and through rockhand handrock.[23] So, for me, standing there awkwardly with my own hand, it seemed moot to decide precise meanings for the hand raised in hail (hello, good-bye, stop, come close, refusal, in- vitation, or move along). In the (negative) space among hands and among rock, there opened intervals, and those intervals contained multitudes. The undecidability or indeterminacy of an interval at the *extended* threshold of response is perhaps what Andre Lepecki, channeling Erin Manning, means by the neologism *leadingfollowing*. Leadingfollowing is how Lepecki describes Manning's (2009, 108) description of the complexities of intraaction in much dance prac- tice, where follower(s) in fact cue leader(s) and a follower can be said, as often as not, to initiate. The same might be said of call and response—where the response is also a call that invites a change in the meaning of the received or recycled hail. In either case—

between the bodies of dancers or in the interval between a call and a response—there is both historicity and virtuality: anything can (have) happen(ed).[24] Responding to Manning, Lepecki (2013, 36) posits the undecidability of leadingfollowing as "dancing in the interval." By dancing in the interval, Lepecki is leadingfollowing the thoughts of Jacques Rancière (2010) for whom the interval is the opening for dissensus, and dissensus is the happening, the taking place, of politics.

In "Living Rocks: Animacy, Performance and the Rock Art of the Kilmartin Region, Argyll, Scotland," Andrew Meirion Jones considers Neolithic rock art to be ongoing performance. But he does not romanticize animacy by virtue of the molecular. Rather, he posits, "prehistoric carvers perceived the rocks—on which the rock art of the region was carved—as animate." Rather than assuming that people imbued the rocks of the region with false agency, he asks that we assume that "people were instead *responding* to the animacy of the rocks" (Jones 2012, 79). Jones is describing an intra-agentic exchange of call and response. In Jones's estimation, perhaps the rocks were hailing, and Neolithic carvers were responding, and Neolithic humans and nonhumans were actively participating—call and response *with* stone that in turn produced another call, to "successive generations visiting the rocks" (Jones 2012, 86), who might, upon their visit, submit the scene to "re-use" (Cochrane and Jones 2012, 9).[25] Here the emphasis shifts off of a generalized claim about the animacy of everything and onto the idea of interstitial relations across varieties of heterogeneous beings engaging in call and response. In this case, animacy, like agency, might be considered to move *among* human and nonhuman in an intra-in-animate weave of call and response-ability. Animacy, here, might be akin to the cut, or the interval, across which we call to each other in intersectional relationways that always open, as Collins and Bilge (2016) suggest, to a shift in perspective, the possibility for politics. Similarly, animacy, here, might be akin to mimesis—the action of becoming through repetition that is not representation but (re)iteration.

Let us return to our future-traveling crew on the starship *Enterprise*
and the rocklife that re-sets the human life-forms upon their own
historical stage. Watching the episode, I heard the rock pronounce
the plant's name as "Exculpia." This turned out to be a mistake. In
the transcript, I found the name written as "Excalbia"—a work easily
misrecognized along the aural fault lines of a homonym. Listening,
I took the planet's name to be a word playing on exculpation, and
thus suggesting "without fault" or, perhaps, fault under erasure.
Exculpatory means, of course, evidence tending to exonerate or
remove blame. Why is Abraham Lincoln played out "again" as
geological life or as ongoing life in geological time? And what part
of that replay concerns fault and its exculpation or reconciliation?
Fault, of course, is a word meaning *both* an extended break in
a body of rock, marked by the displacement and discontinuity
of strata, *and* the bearing of responsibility for unfortunate or
mistaken action.

At a disarmingly awkward moment early in "Savage Curtain,"
Lincoln, only recently arrived on the ship as a living lump of stone,

Figure 2.12. Kirk, Uhura, and Lincoln in "The Savage Curtain," *Star Trek,* season 3,
episode 22.

awkwardly apologizes to Uhura for his impulsive use of the word "Negress." He quickly says, "Oh, forgive me my dear! I know that in my time some used that term as a description of property."

Though Lincoln's gendered phrase "my dear" performs a patronizing dismissal that reminds us how far, in fact, we hadn't come in our so-called bold going future, the script clearly intends this cross-temporal apology to somehow resonate with an audience. But Uhura dismisses his apology cheerfully, just this side of throwing shade: "But why should I object to that term, sir? You see, in our century we've learned not to fear words." Certainly the actress Nichelle Nichols can be seen to be hard at work in this segment of her script, in which a past that hails her at the level of skin hails her again in order for Uhura to dismiss them as "mere words." Nichols's teeth look clenched, however, suggesting it's not quite possible to fully pull off, to felicitously *perform* the future in which, as she effectively tells Lincoln, "words mean nothing." After all, her dismissal of words comes from the bridge of the ship her character serves as Communications Officer, where she spends her hyper-mini-skirted days listening for words to translate across the universe in case those words mean harm! A universe in which, as this and other episodes show, the past is nothing if not irruptive. In any case, what we have here is a lump of land apologizing for the outmodedness of a time when humans considered beings (humans and land alike) as property. This, in a show beamed into American living rooms on the eve of neoliberalism's extensive and ever-expanding privatizations—the becoming private property of everything—is hard to fathom. Is this an acting out, or a working through—completely inchoate though it may be—of the fact that extractive exploitation of land for capital was and is intrainanimated with exploitations of flesh, the "obsolete" yet ongoing violences of so-called primitive accumulation (Coulthard 2014)? Is this an articulation of extractive exploitation as some form of historical creeping lichen? By the close of the episode, Lincoln is made to appear apelike (it's entirely unclear what the makeup artists were attempting here, though perhaps it is all meant to resonate with

Figure 2.13. Lincoln in "The Savage Curtain," *Star Trek,* season 3, episode 22.

the title "savage" as well as with the allusion to theatricality in "curtain"?). At one point, blackened Rock/Lincoln faces the camera in a full frontal close-up that presents him as a bust. He is in full blackface at this point, and says, stone still and staring directly at his future audience, "I was reputed to be a gentle man when I was commander in chief during the four bloodiest years of my country's history. I gave orders that sent one hundred thousand men to their death at the hands of their brothers."

He has been holding on to a stick fashioned into a spear that has a single leaf left, dangling precariously and trembling throughout his speech. Since he is stone still, the trembling leaf is oddly magnified in the frame. Just after Lincoln confesses his culpability in the bloodshed, the actor suddenly looks away from the audience and stares at his hand, also blackened inexplicably. The actor performs a kind of gasp and opens his hand across the screen. In fact, this odd move is performed as if his hand is independent of his body,

Figure 2.14. Lincoln in "The Savage Curtain," *Star Trek,* season 3, episode 22.

as if it might strike him across a fault line in the rock that is his self, or across the history that is not past. His hand trembles now like the leaf as he says, simply, to Kirk, "There is no honorable way to kill."

This bit of confessional, this admission of culpability—is *this* where no man has gone before? The scene reminds viewers of the whiter Land as Lincoln who opened the episode, and his precedent awkward apology for the condition of property at all. After his confession he is barely able, like the leaf, to keep from trembling, but he heads into battle (where he will die trying to save the Vulcan historical forefather Surak, who has also mysteriously materialized from rock). We can be fairly sure that this will not be the last time, as it is not the first time, "Lincoln" "dies." It is entirely appropriate to ask, of course, without recourse to a singular answer, is this a critique of technological "civilization" in the name of the theatrical "savage curtain" or is it a redoing of racializing tropes, hurtling them into our future unremarked? Perhaps it is both/and. Clearly

the very racialization for which rematerialized "Lincoln" apologizes
is far from over and gone, and yet this seems to be part and parcel
of what is being "explored" in an episode that tries, if fails, to go
elsewhere, otherwise.[26] Suffice to say that *Star Trek* approaches
history by standing by, or sidestepping with it via the future, in
an attempt that simultaneously works, faulty though its attempts
may be, to undo the animacy hierarchy between human and
nonhuman. Perhaps this undoing is undone only for the sake of
theatrical alienation—the cheap thrills that would, during commercial breaks, sell hand soap and Jell-O to mid-century consumers.
But we would do well to recall that for Bertolt Brecht, "alienation"
as theatrical technique could also work to open the opportunity for
critical thought and, in the wake of that thought, the potential for
social and political change—the potential for queering habit right
out of its orbit.

Fascinatingly, the *Enterprise*'s inability to parse live and nonlive
doubles, in this episode (as in "Spectre of the Gun," where the *Star
Trek* crew are similarly forced to reenact violent U.S. history), as an
inability to parse past and present as well as a challenge to distinctions between "good" and "evil." As the glowing red hunk of molten
rock says at the close, challenging dyadic worldviews, "You have
failed to demonstrate to me any difference between your philosophies. Your good and your evil use the same methods, achieve the
same results. Do you have an explanation?" And all Kirk can do is
point a finger at the rock and shout angrily that it's rock's fault for
setting the scene and being the ground of the repetitive action!
Petulant, all Kirk wants are "the lives" of his crew. And yet, just what
is live and what is not, what is human and what is nonhuman, what
is old and what is new, is no longer discernible to anyone in the
orbit of the episode.

At the episode's close, with music gently surging, Kirk enigmatically
says, "There is still so much of their work to be done in the galaxy."
Their work? Mineral work? The work in which mineral life forces
settler-colonial humans with their deadly extraction machines
to account for the violences of our future's pasts? We might well

wonder at such life, like Lincoln's, that keeps on living like lichen in the cracks of our medial encounters. The wake of the slave ships of the Middle Passage that keep "us" in their wake, the tracks of the many treks—the many *Star Trek* spinoff ships and fandom slash fantasies "shipping"[27] roles that have catapulted off the earth in search of queer alien life—all seem like waves that keep on waving, quests that keep on questing. A question Tavia Nyong'o (2015) has posed of digitally recombinant *Star Trek* fantasies, such as the erotic pairing of Kirk and Spock or Spock and Uhura, is resonant here:

> Are shippers just digging deeper into homonormative pathologies, or are they displaying the restless and recombinant inventiveness of a connective generation, when they attempt to resolve the real contradictions of race, gender, and sexuality by reimagining slash fiction, beyond the erotic dyad, as a kind of super team?

Or is the answer both/and? To boldly ask what we've asked again and again?

Meanwhile, back on earth and deep underground, a twenty-five-thousand-year-old hand is held in tandem with rock. Might we think of the rockhand handrock as an ongoing gesture rather than an obsolete trace? Might we ask with the gesture perceived as ongoing how to handle our planetary relation-ships differently? How can we approach the *matter* of intrainanimacy with respect for all lifeways that circulate among us all, across vast stretches of time, vast stretches of space, as well as at the tiniest increment of a single quivering leaf or bit of detritus of bone? The Pacific Gyre has been described, oddly enough, as a curtain—emblem of the outmode of theater. "It's sort of like a long floating curtain, which is about five feet above the water and five feet below the water," says Boyan Slat, CEO of the Ocean Cleanup (cited in Raphael 2016). The show that is running at that curtain is also theatrical, dissimulating, brokering an experience of something it is not: "It acts like an artificial coastline where there is no coastline," Slat says. Reference to technologies of mimesis, to "acting like," is how

Slat describes the swirl of afterliving plastics that are the strangely nonvanishing secret of obsolescence. We might also call this odd curtain a continual crisis of brokering. A massive curtain of plastic and discarded detritus of capitalist empire, this "savage curtain" is a primary component of the outmode. In theater, the curtain is always vestigial. And nevertheless, it runs across the bleeding edge of the proscenium arch to open on the old made "new" again, live.

At the close of the *Star Trek* episode, no one aboard the *Enterprise* has any explanation for the rocklife they encountered nor for the futurepast they engaged. It apparently is enough that across our screens, the geologic media as agents of theater mounted their play, and the humans, tongues aflicker, played their part. "There is still so much of *their* work to be done in the galaxy," Kirk muses. And with that, the audience stands by as Kirk simply asks Mr. Sulu to "break us out of orbit." If I listen errantly, I might just get it wrong: break us out of habit. Break us out of habit. I listen and listen again in the fault lines, in the shipping, in the break. The pile of garbage that is the gyre is a curtain that opens only on the oceanic. I imagine, floating there, the plastic gloves I used with Gina in the basement of the archive to touch the flickering mask of tragedy. It's time to think again about handling and shipping and handling again. Indeed, Something's Coming or Something's Going as we hold out our hands in the interstice.

Notes

Many thanks to the many people who have read and commented on drafts of this text in its multiple prior forms, among them Ioana Jucan, Hollis Mickey, Matthew Reason, Christopher Braddock, Paul Rae, and Jennifer Parker-Starbuck. Sections of this essay have been expanded or revised from portions of previous publications included in the bibliography as Schneider (2016, 2017b, 2018).

1   When experience is brokered through media, there can be no "first" time, no originality, given that to be iterative is to be engaged, as with language or physical gesture, in repetition. As Walter Benjamin made clear, there can be no original with technological reproduction, and, perhaps ironically, this is something media share with live performance in general. Parsing "live" media from "nonlive" or "technological" media becomes entangled in assumptions about

what constitutes presence and absence, what recording and what replaying. Despite best efforts to nail down distinctions into solid, nontraversable binaries, the borders between live and nonlive media forms are bloodied, if not completely blurred. See Schneider (2011, 2012).

2   See Stiegler (1998, 143–46) on media as agents of prostheticity that engage what is "put-out-of-range" of the hand (even possibly while being in hand). See the critique by Carrie Noland (2009, 108–9). The length and breadth of the entanglement of theories of the hand with theories of media is well beyond the scope of this essay but informs my thinking here about "the hand" as something of a mediatic *remain.*

3   On the continual crisis of new media, see Chun (2016b, 69–96). On historical definitions of *medium, media, the media,* and *new media,* see Chun (2016a, 3–4). Chun reminds us that in the eighteenth century, "paper was a medium of mass circulation, as was money" (3), and following the money trail backward from the "new" might be one form of media archaeology that finds the bone disk as "medium" of circulation. Obviously, money and paper were performing as intermediaries long before the growth of capitalist industry in the eighteenth-century made circulation (and media) "mass" and tied media, like capitalism, to crisis.

4   The newness of new media might share something with the "discoveries" of prehistory in some interesting ways. Modernity's thrall to the new included the prehistoric. The spread of newness to ancient history as well as to prehistory was, some have argued, a legacy of the birth of modern archaeology that performed "discoveries" of excavation as surprise. Richard H. Armstrong (2006, 31) writes of the "nineteenth century's confrontation with the radical newness of the past that seemed to erupt publicly and scandalously into the pubic imaginary. . . . After all, to be truly modern, in the scientific sense of embracing evolution, meant professing one's antiquity as a member of a primate species." See also Mitchell (2006).

5   For the myriad complications of the rubric "live," and trouble at the borders between so-called animate and so-called inanimate, see Cooper (2008), Chen (2012), and Schneider (2011, 2012).

6   Phillip Auslander (1999) has argued that liveness is an invention of modern technology, and certainly the distinction between so-called mediated and so-called live events is a by-product of modernity and as complicated and in need of undoing as the "old–new" binary. See Schneider (2011) and Cooper (2008). In fact, to call the biobody "live" or only live may be misleading. In addition, more needs to be done to situate Auslander's media-invented liveness with and against the vitalist neoanimism of some new materialism. Is the "reenchantment of the world" underway with current neoanimisms also an "invention" of modern technologies—perhaps an invention of liveness *again*? Some work in this area imagines a "return" to or resurgence of precapitalist and/or indigenous, gift-economy lifeways. The question remains, I think, which works *redress* extractive settler colonialism and which *repeat it,* or vampirically mine again the life from worlds capitalism had marked for consumptive obsolescence (Stiegler 2014; Bennett 2001; 2010; Harvey 2005).

7   On curse tablets and the invisible or inaudible remains of theatrical labor
     cross-temporally, see Johnson (2009).

8   "Stickiness" is an aspect of connection in feminist affect theory that would be
     applicable here. See Schneider (2011, 36–37).

9   See Sarah Jane Cervenak's (2014) introduction to *Wandering: Philosophical
     Performances of Racial and Sexual Freedom.*

10   On "resurgence" of indigenous lifeways and decolonial alternatives to capital-
     colonialism's incessant binary oppositions (that endlessly replay dialectical
     dramas of recognition), see Simpson (2011) and Coulthard (2014).

11   This replacement, subsumption, or interpellation happens "without any suc-
     cession," as Althusser (1971, 175) noted of rituals and habits that preserve
     the status quo and reproduce the conditions for capitalist production. That is,
     obsolescence replicates itself as each "new" form is interpellated. This happens
     without one obsolescence taking the successive place of another. The effect of
     obsolescence is therefore oceanic rather than progressive or dialectical.

12   After all, Stelarc's manifesto proclamations concerning the body's coming ob-
     solescence may now seem more obsolete than the bodies he proclaimed to be
     so (Paffrath and Stelarc 1984). Perhaps he simply missed that the body's obso-
     lescence is nothing new but in fact, ironically, the very mode of its becoming/
     remaining. As an omnivorous obsolescence that renews itself, it may be flesh's
     long-standing given condition.

13   Hands run deep in media theory. Often, however, "hands" are a limiting
     metonym for the singularly agential human animal. In "What Is Called Think-
     ing," Martin Heidegger (1976) famously defines humanness as "the hand,"
     linking hands to thought. Heidegger's worry about technology is precisely that
     the human hand (which is to say, human thought) is in "danger" of obsoles-
     cence. As such, the use of "hands" in theory has often tracked with an animacy
     hierarchy that upholds a biological and humanist bias, one that has also sep-
     arated white European humans from inhuman, racialized others (see Derrida
     1987, 161–96, esp. 173). As such, and ironically, the hand that can grasp a
     tool-in-hand both defines and threatens the category "human" inaugurated by
     in-handedness (Noland 2009). The aim of this essay is not to resolve the ques-
     tion of the humanness or nonhumanness of the hand but to think obliquely,
     stepping to the side of the humanist bias to see what else we can take think
     with our hands when materials, like small bone discs, are passed through and
     among them. If we think of the hand as gesture—moving and moved by the air
     between and among us, for instance—what do we think? If we think with the
     hand as relational, or as intrainanimate and composed in the tactility of the
     nonhuman world (Barad 2012), what do we think?

14   See Coulthard (2014) on the dialectic as a tool of settler colonialism. Troubling
     betweenness and the persistence of the binary in dialectics, see Moten (2003b).

15   One need only recall Wendy Chun's (2011, 170) useful phrase "the enduring
     ephemeral" to access the unwinding of previously solid distinctions between
     disappearance on one hand and remains on the other.

16   Doubtless, Leroi-Gourhan understood that the appearance of the human is the
     appearance of the technical and that the human is invented in the invention

of the tool. However, Noland (2009, 94) argues that the tendency in media theory has been to forget that it is also the body that wields the tool in *gestural* routines of the recombinant body that creates a current "flowing both ways." Neither hand alone nor tool alone but interval—gestic intraspace—where both hand and tool are gesture. It is worth quoting Noland at greater length here. What Stiegler and Leroi-Gourhan's critics in general fail to explore is "(1) if tool-making and manipulation are neither coincident with nor exclusive to human beings, then there is no special purchase to the argument that the human and the technical come into being simultaneously . . . , and (2) if tool-making and manipulation are available to animals and humans alike, it is because their bodies are themselves *sensate* tools. The hand that touches is also the hand that is touched—to recall Husserl's famous image—and thus the first tool is also a gesture that produces kinesthetic, proprioceptive and haptic knowledge" (98).

17 DeForest Kelley, who plays McCoy, does not inflect this line as a question but delivers it as a statement in his performance. In an online transcript copyrighted by CBS, the line is followed by a question mark. Kelley slightly alters other of his lines as well. The dialogue here is lifted from his spoken word in the taped episode. http://www.chakoteya.net/StarTrek/77.htm.

18 Debates on *Star Trek*'s politics are numerous. The claim to white nationalism is made by Daniel Bernardi (1998); counterarguments are made by George A. Gonzalez (2015). For the vexed influence of *Star Trek* on Afrofuturism, see the collection edited by Anderson and Jones (2016).

19 From *Star Trek*'s third season, see not only "Savage Curtain" (first aired March 7, 1969) but also "The Spectre of the Gun," episode 6, first aired October 25, 1968, for alien history reenactments in the future.

20 Coulthard (2014) always couples the word *colonial* with the word *capital,* as he sees the two systems of exploration and exploitation as inextricably entwined. Apropos of (media) archaeology, exploration and exploitation can also be conjoined, in his writing, with excavation. I follow his lead in this essay throughout.

21 For Bergson (2007, 165–68), because multiplicity makes up the unity of duration, duration is essentially heterogeneous and simultaneous, and thus one must reverse habitual modes of thought and place oneself within duration by intuition.

22 See Schneider and Ruprecht (2017) for commentary on the hail in relationship to the activation of ideology. See also Schneider (2018) for a closer engagement with the possibilities of cross-temporal hails.

23 Jean Clottes and David Lewis-Williams (1998) literally "set out to encounter the shamans" (23) by visiting Paleolithic caves where the "shamanistic potency" of images is a "life force" (23) and where the panels are not "mere pictures" but "gateways to the spirit world," a "stage set awaiting the shamanic actors" (35). Note that they seek to encounter the shamans themselves, by virtue of a live passage *through* the "gateway" of their art. This view, which is sometimes manifested in writing that bears the ecstatic flavor of the "trance" it seeks to explore, has been criticized by Paul Bahn (2008, 15), who writes that it represents

a "great leap backwards." Useful books for situating heated debates in the study of cave art are Mats Rosengren (2012) and Gregory Curtis (2006). Yann Montelle's (2009, 50-51) *Paleolithic Performance: The Emergence of Theatricality as a Social Practice* looks to the artwork for "gestural patterns" learned through "hands on" experience that can be "reactivated" for excavation by live bodily knowledges.

24 Ironically, the interval is provoked to thought by collapsing the literal space between words, as in *leadingfollowing, callresponse, subjectobject, livingdead, manwoman,* or *intrainanimate.* This may be a redistribution of the sensible that invites a queering or disorientation of normative alignments but also, again perhaps ironically, mirrors modes of address in the digital age where the size or speed of intervals has in some cases been rapidly diminishing (think of publicprivate), even as other gaps have exponentially grown (think of the growing gap between rich and poor).

25 Jones (2012, 87) argues that rock carving is a "performance" and participates in an "interconnected series of performances." Though he distinguishes performance from representation in the introduction to the volume, cowritten with Andrew Cochrane, the suggestion is also made that such work might be "both representations and performances," stressing the "performative nature of representation" (Cochrane and Jones 2012, 3).

26 The series *Star Trek* is also responsible for an early, much-noted interracial kiss, though it is an enforced one, performed through coercion in outer space between Kirk and Uhura within a reenactment of ancient Greece that looks more like ancient Rome in an episode titled "Plato's Stepchildren." That episode, like "Savage Curtain," simply boggles the mind.

27 The word *shipping,* shortened from relationship, is used in fandom to signify the desire by fans to place two or more characters or actors in a relationship, often romantic. This is also known as *slash.*

References

Agamben, Giorgio. 2011. *The Kingdom and the Glory: For a Theological Genealogy of Economy and Government.* Palo Alto, Calif.: Stanford University Press.

Alföldi-Rosenbaum, Elizabeth. 1971. "The Finger Calculus in Antiquity and the Middle Ages: Studies in Roman Game Counters." *Frühmittelalterliche Studien* 5: 1–9.

Althusser, Louis. 1971. "Ideology and Ideological State Apparatuses," translated by Ben Brewster. In *Lenin and Philosophy and Other Essays,* 127–86. New York: Monthly Review Press.

Anderson, Reynaldo, and Charles E. Jones. 2016. *Afrofuturism 2.0.* London: Lexington Books.

Armstrong, Richard H. 2006. *A Compulsion for Antiquity: Freud and the Ancients.* Ithaca, N.Y.: Cornell University Press.

Auslander, Philip. 1999. *Liveness.* New York: Routledge.

Bahn, Paul. 2008. "Holding onto Smoke: Wishful Thinking vs Common Sense in Rock

Art Interpretation." In *Iconography without Texts,* edited by Paul Taylor, 15–24. London: Warburg Institute.

Barad, Karen. 2003. "Posthumanist Performativity: Toward an Understanding of How Matter Comes to Matter." *Signs* 28, no. 3: 801–31.

Barad, Karen. 2007. *Meeting the Universe Halfway: Quantum Physics and the Entanglement of Matter and Meaning.* Durham, N.C.: Duke University Press.

Barad, Karen. 2012. "On Touching—the Inhuman That Therefore I Am." *Differences* 23, no. 3: 206–23.

Benjamin, Walter. 1969. *Illuminations.* Translated by Harry Zohn. New York: Schocken Books.

Bennett, Jane. 2001. *The Enchantment of Modern Life: Attachments, Crossings, and Ethics.* Princeton, N.J.: Princeton University Press.

Bennett, Jane. 2010. *Vibrant Matter.* Baltimore: Johns Hopkins University Press.

Bergson, Henri. 2007. *The Creative Mind: An Introduction to Metaphysics.* Translated by Mabelle L. Andison. New York: Dover.

Bernardi, Daniel. 1998. *Star Trek and History: Race-ing toward a White Future.* New Brunswick, N.J.: Rutgers University Press.

Bernstein, Robin. 2009. "Dances with Things: Material Culture and the Performance of Race." *Social Text* 27, no. 4: 68.

Bieber, Margarete. 1961. *The History of the Greek and Roman Theater.* Princeton, N.J.: Princeton University Press.

Butler, Judith. 1988. "Performative Acts and Gender Constitution: An Essay in Phenomenology and Feminist Theory." *Theatre Journal* 40, no. 4: 519–31.

Caillois, Roger. (1935) 1984. "Mimicry and Legendary Psychasthenia." Translated by John Shepley. *October* 31: 12–32.

Cervenak, Sarah Jane. 2014. *Wandering: Philosophical Performances of Racial and Sexual Freedom.* Durham, N.C.: Duke University Press.

Chen, Mel Y. 2012. *Animacies: Biopolitics, Racial Mattering, and Queer Affect.* Durham, N.C.: Duke University Press.

Chun, Wendy. 2011. *Programmed Visions: Software and Memory.* Cambridge, Mass.: MIT Press.

Chun, Wendy. 2016a. "Did Somebody Say New Media?" In *Old Media, New Media,* edited by Wendy Hui Kyong Chun and Anna Watkins Fisher, 1–16. New York: Routledge.

Chun, Wendy. 2016b. *Updating to Remain the Same: Habitual New Media.* Cambridge, Mass.: MIT Press.

Clottes, Jean, and David Lewis-Williams. 1998. *The Shamans of Prehistory: Trance and Magic in the Painted Caves.* Translated by Sophie Hawkes. New York: Harry N. Abrams.

Cochrane, Andrew, and Andrew Meirion Jones. 2012. "Visualising the Neolithic: An Introduction." In *Visualising the Neolithic,* edited by Andrew Cochrane and Andrew Meirion Jones, 1–14. Oxford: Oxbow Books.

Collins, Patricia Hill, and Sirma Bilge. 2016. *Intersectionality.* New York: Polity Press.

Cooper, Melinda E. 2008. *Life as Surplus: Biotechnology and Capitalism in the Neoliberal Era.* Seattle: University of Washington Press.

Coulthard, Glen Sean. 2014. *Red Skins, White Masks: Rejecting the Colonial Politics of Recognition.* Minneapolis: University of Minnesota Press.

Curtis, Gregory. 2006. *The Cave Painters—Probing the Mysteries of the World's First Artists.* New York: Alfred A. Knopf.

de Certeau, Michel. 1984. *The Practice of Everyday Life.* Berkeley: University of California Press.

DeFrantz, Thomas F., and Anita Gonzalez. 2014. "Introduction: From Negro Expression to Black Performance." In *Black Performance Theory,* edited by Thomas F. DeFranz and Anita Gonzalez, 1–18. Durham, N.C.: Duke University Press.

Deleuze, Gilles. 1994. *Difference and Repetition.* New York: Columbia University Press.

Deleuze, Gilles, and Félix Guattari. 1987. *A Thousand Plateaus: Capitalism and Schizophrenia.* Translated by Brian Massumi. Minneapolis: University of Minnesota Press.

Derrida, Jacques. 1987. "Geschlecht II: Heidegger's Hand," in *Deconstruction and Philosophy: The Texts of Jacques Derrida,* ed. John Sallis. Chicago: University of Chicago Press.

Derrida, Jacques, and Gianni Vattimo. 1998. *Religion.* Palo Alto, Calif.: Stanford University Press.

Feffer, John. 2015. "What Can 'Star Trek' Teach Us about American Exceptionalism?" *Nation,* September.

Gonzalez, George A. 2015. *The Politics of Star Trek.* New York: Palgrave Macmillan.

Gonzalez Rice, Karen. 2016. *Long Suffering: American Endurance Art as Prophetic Witness.* Ann Arbor: University of Michigan Press.

Greenblatt, Stephen. 1988. *Shakespearean Negotiations: The Circulation of Social Energy in Renaissance England.* Berkeley and Los Angeles: University of California Press

Greven, David. 2009. *Gender and Sexuality in Star Trek: Allegories of Desire in the Television Series and Films.* New York: McFarland.

Haraway, Donna. 2003. *Companion Species Manifesto.* Chicago: Prickly Paradigm Press.

Harvey, Graham. 2005. *Animism: Respecting the Living World.* New York: Columbia University Press.

Heathfield, Adrian. 2015. *Out of Now: The Lifeworks of Tehching Hsieh.* Cambridge, Mass.: MIT Press.

Ingold, Tim. 2006. "Rethinking the Animate, Reanimating Thought." *Ethnos: Journal of Anthropology* 71, no. 1: 9–20.

Johnson, Odai. 2009. "Unspeakable Histories: Terror, Spectacle and Genocidal Memory." *Modern Language Quarterly* 70, no. 1: 97–116.

Jones, Andrew Meirion. 2012. "Living Rocks: Animacy, Performance and the Rock Art of the Kilmartin Region." In *Visualising the Neolithic,* edited by Andrew Cochrane and Andrew Meirion Jones, 79–88. Oxford: Oxbow Books.

Kapchan, Deborah. 2007. *Traveling Spirit Masters: Moroccan Gnawa Trance and Music in the Global Marketplace.* Middletown, Conn.: Wesleyan University Press.

Keller, Mary. 2001. *The Hammer and the Flute: Women, Power, and Spirit Possession.* Baltimore: Johns Hopkins University Press.

Lepecki, Andre. 2013. "From Partaking to Initiating: Leadingfollowing as Dance's (A-personal) Political Singularity." In *Dance, Politics and Co-Immunity: Current*

Perspectives on Politics and Communities in the Arts, edited by Sefan Holscher and Philipp Schulte, 23–40. Chicago: University of Chicago Press.

Manning, Erin. 2009. "The Elasticity of the Almost." In *Planes of Composition: Dance, Theory, and the Global,* edited by Andre Lepecki and Jenn Joy, 107–22. London: Seagull Press.

Merleau-Ponty, Maurice. 2012. *The Phenomenology of Perception.* Translated by Donald A. Landes. New York: Routledge.

Mignolo, Walter. 2005. *The Idea of Latin America.* London: Blackwell.

Mitchell, W. J. T. 2006. *What Do Pictures Want? The Lives and Loves of Images.* Chicago: University of Chicago Press.

Mitchell, W. J. T., and Mark B. N. Hansen. 2010. *Critical Terms for Media Studies.* Chicago: University of Chicago Press.

Montelle, Yann. 2009. *Paleoperformance: The Emergence of Theatricality as Social Practice.* New York: Seagull Books.

Moten, Fred. 2003a. *In the Break: The Aesthetics of the Black Radical Tradition.* Minneapolis: University of Minnesota Press.

Moten, Fred. 2003b. "Not in Between: Lyric Painting, Visual History, and the Postcolonial Future." *TDR: A Journal of Performance Studies* 47, no 1: 127–48.

Muñoz, José Esteban. 1999. *Disidentifications: Queers of Color and the Performance of Politics.* Minneapolis: University of Minnesota Press.

Noland, Carrie. 2009. *Agency and Embodiment: Performing Gestures, Producing Culture.* Cambridge, Mass.: Harvard University Press.

Nyong'o, Tavia. 2015. "The Shipped and the Bereft, or, Seven Backward Glances That Won't Turn You to Salt." *Bullyblogger* (blog), March 6. https://bullybloggers.word press.com/2015/03/06/the-shipped-and-the-bereft-or-seven-backward-glances -that-wont-turn-you-to-salt/.

Paffrath, James D., and Stelarc, eds. 1984. *Obsolete Body/Suspensions/Stelarc.* New York: J. P. Publications.

Parikka, Jussi. 2015. *A Geology of Media.* Minneapolis: University of Minnesota Press.

Rancière, Jacques. 2010. *Dissensus: On Politics and Aesthetics.* London: Continuum.

Raphael, T. J. 2016. "Meet the 22-Year-Old with a Big Idea for Cleaning Up the Great Pacific Garbage Patch." Public Radio International, August 17. https://www.pri.org/ stories/2016-08-17/meet-22-year-old-big-idea-cleaning-great-pacific-garbage -patch.

Roach, Joseph. 1996. *Cities of the Dead: Circum-Atlantic Performance.* New York: Columbia University Press.

Rosengren, Mats. 2012. *Cave Art, Perception, and Knowledge.* New York: Palgrave Macmillan.

Schneider, Rebecca. 2011. *Performing Remains: Art and War in Times of Theatrical Reenactment.* New York: Routledge.

Schneider, Rebecca. 2012. "It Seems as If I Am Dead: Zombie Capitalism and Theatrical Labor." *TDR: A Journal of Performance Studies* 56, no 4: 150–62.

Schneider, Rebecca. 2016. "Bone Theatre." In *Experiencing liveness in contemporary performance,* edited by Matthew Reason and Anja Mølle Lindelof. London: Routledge.

Schneider, Rebecca, and Lucia Ruprecht. 2017a. "In Our Hands: Toward an Ethics of Gestural Response-ability, Rebecca Schneider in Conversation with Lucia Ruprecht." *Performance Philosophy* 2, no. 3.

Schneider, Rebecca. 2017b. "Intra-inanimations." In *Animism in Art and Performance,* edited by Christopher Braddock, 191–212. New York: Palgrave Macmillan.

Schneider, Rebecca. 2018. "That the Past May Yet Have Another Future: Gesture in the Times of Hands Up." *Theatre Journal* 70, no. 3.

Serres, Michel. 2013. *The Parasite.* Translated by Lawrence R. Schehr. Minneapolis: University of Minnesota Press.

Sharpe, Christina. 2016. *In the Wake: On Blackness and Being.* Durham, N.C.: Duke University Press.

Silverman, Kaja. 1995. *Threshold of the Visible World.* New York: Routledge.

Simpson, Leanne. 2011. *Dancing on Our Turtle's Back: Stories of Nishnaabeg Re-creation, Resurgence, and a New Emergence.* Winnipeg, Manitoba: Arbeiter Ring.

Spielman, Loren R. 2012. "Playing Roman in Jerusalem: Jewish Attitudes toward Sport and Spectacle during the Second Temple Period." In *Jews in the Gym: Judaism, Sports, and Athletics,* edited by Leonard Greenspoon, 1–24. Purdue, Ill.: Purdue University Press.

St. Clair, Archer. 2003. *Carving as Craft: Paletine East and the Greco-Roman Bone and Ivory Carving Tradition.* Baltimore: Johns Hopkins University Press.

Stiegler, Bernard. 1998. *Technics and Time,* vol. 1, *The Fault of Epimetheus.* Translated by Richard Beardsworth and George Collins. Palo Alto, Calif.: Stanford University Press.

Stiegler, Bernard. 2014. *The Re-enchantment of the World.* Translated by Trevor Arthur. New York: Bloomsbury.

Taussig, Michael. 1993. *Mimesis and Alterity.* New York: Routledge.

Tischleder, Babette B., and Sarah Wasserman. 2015. Introduction to *Cultures of Obsolescence: History, Materiality, and the Digital Age,* edited by Babette B. Tischleder and Sarah Wasserman. New York: Palgrave Macmillan.

United Nations News Center. 2015. "UN Environment Chief Warns of 'Tsunami' of e-Waste at Conference on Chemical Treaties." May 4.

Wise, Jennifer. 2000. *Dionysus Writes: The Invention of Theatre in Ancient Greece.* Ithaca, N.Y.: Cornell University Press.

Žižek, Slavoj. 1992. *Looking Awry: An Introduction to Jacques Lacan through Popular Culture.* Cambridge, Mass.: MIT Press.

Authors

Ioana B. Jucan is a researcher and artist working at the intersection of theater and performance, philosophy, and new media. Several of her performance texts are collected in her book *Cosmology of Worlds Apart.*

Jussi Parikka is professor in technological culture and aesthetics at University of Southampton. He is the author of *A Slow Contemporary Violence* (2016)*, A Geology of Media* (Minnesota, 2015), *The Anthrobscene* (Minnesota, 2014), *What Is Media Archaeology?* (2012)*, Insect Media: An Archaeology of Animals and Technology* (Minnesota, 2010), and *Digital Contagions: A Media Archaeology of Computer Viruses* (2007).

Rebecca Schneider is professor of theater arts and performance studies at Brown University. She is the author of *Theatre and History* (2014), *Performing Remains: Art and War in Times of Theatrical Reenactment* (2011), and *The Explicit Body in Performance* (1997).